The faith of
Generation Y

Praise for *Making Sense of Generation Y* (2006)

'Making Sense of Generation Y *is astonishing. Putting it bluntly, it suggests that many of our assumptions about young people, their world view and quest for spirituality are wrong. This has implications for the future of mission, youth ministry and the Church. A must read.*'

Jonny Baker, Mission Adviser for Youth and Emerging Church, Church Mission Society

'*This important book does us a great service in giving us an insight into the world view of* Generation Y *... and I commend it as a starting point for those wanting to proclaim Christ afresh in this generation.*'

Dr John Sentamu, Archbishop of York

The faith of
Generation Y

Sylvia Collins-Mayo, Bob Mayo, Sally Nash
with Christopher Cocksworth

 CHURCH HOUSE
PUBLISHING

Church House Publishing
Church House
Great Smith Street
London SW1P 3AZ

ISBN 978 0 7151 4206 6

Published 2010 by Church House Publishing

The opinions expressed in this book are those of the author and do not necessarily reflect the official policy of the General Synod or The Archbishops' Council of the Church of England.

Cover design by Andy Stonehouse

Typeset in Rotis Semi Sans by RefineCatch Limited, Bungay, Suffolk

Printed in England by CPI Antony Rowe, Chippenham, Wiltshire

Contents

Contents

About the authors

Dr Sylvia Collins-Mayo is Principal Lecturer in Sociology at Kingston University. She completed her PhD on young people's faith at the University of Surrey in 1997. Her post-doctoral research interests have continued to focus on youth religion with particular reference to the everyday faith of young people from Christian backgrounds. She is co-author of *Making Sense of Generation Y* (CHP, 2006) and co-editor of *Religion and Youth* (Ashgate, 2010).

The Revd Dr Bob Mayo is the vicar of St Stephen's Church, Shepherd's Bush, is a Trustee of the Salmon Youth Centre in Bermondsey, and is the chaplain of Queens Park Rangers. He was previously Director of the Cambridge Centre of Youth Ministry. His other publications include *Gospel Exploded* (SPCK, 1996), *Ambiguous Evangelism* (SPCK, 2004) and *Divorce – A challenge to the Church* (BRF, 2008) and he is co-author of *Making Sense of Generation Y* (CHP, 2006). He also regularly contributes to the *Church of England Newspaper.*

Dr Sally Nash is Director of the Midlands Centre for Youth Ministry and has been involved in the Christian youth work field for over 25 years. She is currently researching sustainable Christian youth work practice and is involved in the support and management of two fresh expressions for young adults. Sally is a Trustee of both Frontier Youth Trust and the Sophia Network and part of the Ministries Forum for the Diocese of Birmingham. As well as *Skills for Collaborative Ministry* (SPCK, 2008) and *Tools for Reflective Ministry* (SPCK, 2009), she has written Grove Booklets on *Sustaining your Spirituality* and *Supervising Youth Workers* (with Malcolm Herbert) and has written articles on a variety of topics.

The Revd Dr Christopher Cocksworth is Bishop of Coventry. Formerly Principal of Ridley Hall, Cambridge, he has been involved in theological education for a number of years. After various publications in the area of worship and ministry, his latest book is *Holding Together: Gospel, Church and Spirit – the essentials of Christian identity* (Canterbury Press, 2008). He has five Generation Y children.

Introduction

In 1989 communism collapsed with the destruction of the Berlin Wall. In 2009 the banking system fractured due to a worldwide crisis of confidence in the financial markets. In between times have come 'Generation Y', born during the 1980s and 1990s and reaching their teens and early adulthood at the beginning of the 21st century. With the global credit crunch, 20 years of uninterrupted economic growth came to an end and an unprecedented burden of national debt was placed on the future working shoulders of young people. Francis Fukuyama's (1992) prophecy that the collapse of communism would mark the 'end of history' has been shown to be at fault.

The 9/11 terrorist destruction of the World Trade Centre in New York in 2001, the invasion of Iraq in 2003 and the London bombings of July 2005 have helped to shape a new world order of which young people are a part. So too have environmental concerns brought into stark relief by the 2004 Indian Ocean tsunami and the destruction of New Orleans by Hurricane Katrina in 2005. In the face of these problems, the inauguration of Barack Obama in January 2009 as the first Black President of the United States seemed an auspicious moment that struck a chord of hope across much of the Western world, for young and old alike.

A generation is defined by the key social, political and economic events experienced during its youth and which come to shape its collective approach to public and private life in adulthood. Generational labels act as convenient shorthand by which to refer to some of the distinctive characteristics different birth cohorts take on. Like any shorthand they gloss over much complexity and diversity, but they at least allow us to get a handle on some of the salient features. For example, the post war 'Baby Boomer Generation' (b. ~ 1946–1963) is associated with the counter-culture movement of the 1960s with its liberalization of social attitudes, its political activism, idealism and optimism. For Generation X (b.~ 1964–1981) which followed, the economic downturn of 1970s, the ideals of individualism and consumption of the 1980s, the rising divorce rates and social problems that came as a legacy to Boomer liberalism are some of the significant factors which have led commentators to describe GenXers as pessimistic and pragmatic (Richter and Francis 1998:48).

Our interest in this book is with Generation Y (born about 1982 onwards). Some of the events which will shape this generation include those mentioned above, others are yet to happen. Our task is not to speculate about what these might be but to consider the resources of faith with which today's young people will face their future. One thing is clear: Generation Y growing up in Britain has had less contact with the Church than any previous generation in living memory. What place then, does Christianity have as a source of meaning, hope and purpose for young people? What is the faith of Generation Y?

In this book we discuss the findings of research conducted over the last five years with young people in England who attended Christian youth and community work projects. We were particularly interested in young people who were not practising Christians nor members of other world faiths; such young people are in the majority in the English population. We wondered what form their everyday faith takes, how they develop their faith and what the consequences of their faith are for daily living. We were especially interested in the effects of the Christian youth work they participated in and whether or not it raised their 'Christian consciousness'. After all, for young people who rarely if ever go to church services, such youth work might be one of the few chances they have to engage with Christianity.

In order to draw out the nuances of the answer to our research questions we have listened in detail to young people's views and personal stories. This was intensive work which necessarily put a limit on the number of young people we could include in our study. Nevertheless, as we explain in chapter 2, we are confident that our findings help to shed light on what lies behind some the beliefs, attitudes and opinions expressed in more statistically representative social surveys, such as those which we also discuss herein. We therefore offer our book as a contribution to the wider debate on young people's religious and spiritual inclinations which make up the faith of Generation Y.

The shape of this book

Our book is divided into two parts reflecting two disciplinary perspectives – sociology and theology. By approaching the study through two lenses we are in a position to situate and reflect upon the attitudes, beliefs and practices which constitute young people's relationship to Christianity and provide an understanding for points of engagement between Church, culture and individuals in late modern society.

By dividing the book into two parts we also recognize that readers have different interests in the faith of Generation Y. Some will be interested in our findings as a comment on the nature of youth religion and, as such, as a contribution to wider sociological debates about the place of religion in contemporary society – Part 1 is for them. Others more interested in practical theology will want to 'cut to the chase' and go straight to Chapter 6 for a summary of our findings and then consider what they might mean from a theological point of view and their implications for mission and ministry – Part 2 is for them. The shape of the book is therefore as follows:

Part One
In Part One, we adopt a sociological perspective to provide the reader with an empirically grounded account of young people's everyday faith. First we set out the background theory (Chapter 1) and context (Chapter 2) of the research. We then go on to consider our findings in terms of young people's faith and its relationship to Christianity (Chapter 3), the processes of faith transmission as experienced by our young people (Chapter 4) and the relevance of Christian faith for them in day to day life (Chapter 5). Chapter 6 summarizes the key sociological points from Chapters 3, 4 and 5.

Part Two
In Part Two we take up our second lens and consider the evidence from a theological point of view (Chapter 7) and the implications of the findings for mission (Chapter 8).

Epilogue
The last word is given over to Bishop Christopher Cocksworth in the Epilogue (Chapter 9), in which he reflects on our study from his perspective as a theologian.

Books of this nature cannot be written without the help and support of numerous individuals along the way. To them we owe our deepest thanks. First, we thank Gordon Izatt and also the Council of Ridley Hall who made the research possible. Then the young people and youth workers who must remain anonymous for the purposes of confidentiality, but without whom we would have nothing to say. Third, our advisory team and those who supported us in many ways throughout the project, in particular: Chris Rose, Deirdre Brower

Latz, Richard Bromley, Louise Bromley, Colin MacRae, Gill Benson, Paul Nash, the staff at Ridley Hall Cambridge, and colleagues at Kingston University and St John's College Nottingham. Finally, to those who have commented upon, and helped us to iron out, the manuscript especially Lynda Barley and our other reviewers.

PART ONE:
SOCIOLOGICAL PERSPECTIVE

1

Faith, memory and young people

'I wouldn't say I was a Christian now, I just pray really. Sometimes you just have to have faith in yourself and try to do things by yourself.' So says Karen, a 20 year old woman living in London who had been brought up as a Christian but no longer sees herself in that way. Karen's statement takes us to the heart of this book – young people's relationship to the Christian faith at the beginning of the 21st century. What interest do young people have in Christianity? How do social influences inform their Christian consciousness? Does belief in God or a Christian identity make any difference to them? These are pressing questions not just for the Church concerned with young people's wellbeing and the future of Christianity, but also for social commentators interested in the changing nature of religion and spirituality in contemporary Britain. We shed light on these questions by drawing on the views of over 300 young people (8 to 23 year olds) who have participated in one of 34 different Christian youth and community outreach projects around England over the past five years. Our focus is particularly on those young people who rarely, if ever, go to church but who also do not belong to any other world faith. These 'unchurched' and 'dechurched'[1] young people make up the majority of teenagers and young adults in England yet we know relatively little about their 'everyday faith' – that is to say, the faith that goes on 'outside organized religious events and institutions' in the mundane routines of ordinary life and the periodic highs and lows along the way (Ammerman 2007:5). Where, if at all, does the Christian tradition fit in?

Down but not out!

Gone are the days when Britain could be characterized undisputedly as a 'Christian country'. Voas (2003) draws attention to the fact that evidence from opinion polls, church attendance surveys and official statistics all point to a society that is moving away from Christianity in its day-to-day beliefs and practices. Young people in particular are less likely to engage with the Christian faith than older people. We can see the extent of disengagement if we look at some of the statistics around religious affiliation, churchgoing and belief.

Religious affiliation

When people were asked 'What is your religion?' in the 2001 national census, 72% of Britons, and 62% of 16 to 34 year olds, replied 'Christian' (ONS 2006). This surely was good news from the Church's point of view – Christianity may be down but it was far from out. More recently, however, the 2006 British Social Attitudes Survey which asked the more engaged question 'Do you regard yourself as *belonging* to any particular religion?' (emphasis added) found only 47% of adults felt this way about Christianity (Park et al 2008:346). For 18 to 24 year olds the figure stood at just 27%, leaving a sizeable majority (59%) who felt they did not belong to any religion at all (NCSR 2008).[2]

To say one 'belongs' to a religion does perhaps imply a higher degree of commitment than people are normally prepared to admit to. It suggests that there is some sort of emotional tie which may well fluctuate according to mood or circumstance. A more formal measure of affiliation often associated with children and young people but not so dependent on feelings, is the number of baptisms and confirmations conducted each year. Here we can note that just over half of all children born in the United Kingdom in the 1990s were baptized (primarily into the Church of England, but also into the Roman Catholic Church and others). For those born between 2000 and 2006 the figure fell to two-fifths (Brierley 2008:4.2). It seems from this that fewer and fewer young people are being brought up in households with religiously inclined parents, or at least with parents who wish to seal the gift of faith to their children. Of course, some parents opt for a thanksgiving service instead of baptism.[3] Nevertheless, for increasing numbers of new parents it appears to be the case that no religious ceremony is needed at all to mark the birth of a child.[4]

Just as baptism rates have declined, so too have confirmations. Church of England figures show the number of confirmations in 1980 was 98,000; in 1990 there were 60,000; and by 2007 the figure had fallen to 28,000[5] (Church of England 2009). Moreover, fewer confirmation candidates are coming forward in their teens. In 1976, 63% of confirmations were of young people aged 12 to 19 years. In 2006 only 37% of candidates were teenagers; the rest were older or younger (Church of England 2008).

Religious practice

Of course just because young people have been baptized or identify themselves as 'Christian' does not mean they are religiously engaged. It is no secret, for instance, that relatively few people in the general population are regular churchgoers if 'regular' means going to church at least once a month. A representative survey of 7,000 adults (16 years and over) commissioned by Tearfund in 2006 found that 15% of people in the United Kingdom claimed to be regular churchgoers; for 16 to 24 year olds the figure fell to 10% (around 731,000 young people). By way of contrast, 45% of 16 to 24 year olds said they had 'never been to church and were unlikely to do so' (Ashworth and Farthing 2007:9). This is not good news for the maintenance of the Christian faith.

Self-reports of church attendance, however, are notoriously unreliable (Voas 2003). They are often subject to over-reporting on the part of adults (Hadaway et al 1993) and possibly under-reporting on the part of young people who fear that churchgoing is not 'cool' (Vincett and Collins-Mayo, 2010). The English Church Census therefore adopts a method of head counting instead, and for 2005 reported that on a 'typical' Sunday around 6.3% of the English population were to be found in church (Brierley, 2006:12). Of these, 6% were young people aged 11 to 14 years and 5% aged 15 to 19 (356,000 young people altogether). Those in their twenties made up a further 7% (230,600 people). This makes teenagers the smallest group in the church. To put it rather more starkly, Brierley points out that 49% of churches in England had *no* 11 to 14 year olds in their congregation on the day of the survey, and 59% had no 15 to 19 year olds.

Considering trends, between 1998 and 2005 the number of 11 to 14 year olds in church fell by 11%; for 15 to 19 year olds the drop was 27%; and for 20 to 29 year olds there was a fall of 29% (Brierley 2006:112, 114). Brierley brings this rate of decline into perspective, however, when he says the 'catastrophic drop among those under 15 in the 1990s has slowed considerably to a much smaller annual rate of loss between 1998 and 2005' (2006:115). Cold comfort indeed!

Rates of church participation and change do vary according to gender, ethnicity and class background. Traditionally it has been the case that girls and women are more likely to go to church than boys and men. This continues to be the case overall, but the gap between the genders is decreasing as women and girls become less devout. In fact, the 2005 English Church Census data records that the number of young men (15 to 19 year olds) in church at the time of the survey actually outnumbered the number of young women (Brierley 2006:130).

One of the reasons why the decline in church attendance was not as 'catastrophic' between 1998 and 2005 as it was for the earlier 1990s was because the Black and Asian population increased and went to church in relatively high numbers compared to the White population. People of African and Caribbean origin, for example, made up around 3.8% of the English population in 2005, but constituted 10% of the English churchgoing population (Brierley 2006). In fact, in inner London there are more Black churchgoers than White. Most Black churchgoers attend Pentecostal churches, but around 8% of Anglicans, Roman Catholics and Baptists in England are of African or Caribbean decent. Of particular relevance to our study is the fact that Black youth are slightly more inclined to be churchgoers than their White peers (Brierley 2006:101).

When it comes to class, data from Francis' (2001) *Teenage Religion and Values Survey* collected during the 1990s[6] suggests that 13 to 15 year olds from working class backgrounds hold less favourable attitudes towards the Church and are less likely to be churchgoers than their middle class peers. 55% of working class young people in Francis' survey thought 'Church is boring' compared to 11% from middle class professional backgrounds. 37% of working class young people thought religious leaders do a good job compared to 42% of middle class young people. On the other hand, young people from socially deprived backgrounds[7] are more likely to be open to 'both traditional religion and to non-traditional religion' (Francis and Robbins 2005:90). It may be the case that although institutional religion is not appealing to this group of young people, private spirituality is more so (Vincett and Collins-Mayo 2010).

Religious belief

While religious participation is generally low, one of the features of modern Britain is that belief in the transcendent or supernatural (God or otherwise) continues, although, along with the decline in church attendance, traditional Christian beliefs are becoming less common. A 2007 YouGov poll found that 18% of 18 to 29 year olds believed 'in a personal God who created the world and hears my prayers' (compared to 22% of the population overall); 7% believed 'in a God who created everything but then left us to get on with it' (6% overall); and 24% believed 'in "something" but I'm not sure what' (26% overall). Only 16% of 18 to 29 year olds said they were atheist and 12% agnostic. 13% did not know what to believe and had not given it much thought (YouGov 2007).

The Teenage Religion and Values Survey (Francis 2001) also indicates that teenagers are selective in their approach to Christian belief. Young people in that survey were less likely to agree with biblical statements (such as 'Jesus really rose from the dead' or 'God made the world in six days and rested on the seventh') than they were to agree with more general statements ('I believe in God'). They were more likely to accept the 'nicer' aspects of Christian belief than the uncomfortable parts (belief in God was more popular than belief in the devil, and belief in life after death more popular than belief in a God who punishes wrong-doers). It was also clear from this survey that large numbers of young people were uncertain about what they believed. Like the 13% in the YouGov poll above, they may well have not given religious beliefs much thought.

Generational change

The above suggests a fair degree of disengagement from Christianity in England, particularly among young people. It could, of course, be argued that young people are less religious than older people because they have not yet had to deal with life situations which make great demands on faith or test their capacity to 'go on'. We shall see throughout our discussion that young people do in fact have a great deal to cope with and require a certain amount of 'faith' to get by, but this is not necessarily *religious* faith. Studies which have addressed the significance of aging effects versus generational decline in religiosity indicate that the latter is a significant factor.

Voas and Crockett (2005) analysed the British Household Panel Survey which includes both longitudinal and cross sectional data for adults aged 18 and above. They conclude that while some individuals may get more religious as they go through life, on the whole most people do not. From their research on 7 to 16 year olds, Kay and Francis (1996) suggest that throughout the years of compulsory schooling young people become less positive toward Christianity and do not change much after that. 'Growing up means becoming indifferent to religion' (1996:31) they argue. Changes in young people's cognitive abilities no doubt have an impact on how young people think about Christian ideas as they grow up. However, for Kay and Francis the main explanation for religious decline during this period is that young people get socialized into an adult world where Christianity is largely irrelevant to day-to-day living. Only by young people retaining contact with church-related groups, they suggest, is the decline likely to be slowed. Our research supports this conclusion.

Bottoming out

While generational decline in Christian engagement is apparent in Britain (and Western Europe), there is also some evidence to suggest a 'bottoming out' of the downward slide. Brierley's title for the 2005 English Church Census report *Pulling Out of the Nose Dive* is perhaps on the optimistic side, but reflects the observation that the loss of young people from church was less at the start of the new millennium than for the early 1990s leading up to it. Voas' (2009) analysis of the 2002/3 European Values Survey indicates that for the *least* religious countries in Europe the drop in levels of religiosity amongst cohorts born after 1960 is less than the decline between previous generations. Francis notes that from 1974 to 1994, 11 to 16 year olds held increasingly negative attitudes toward Christianity, but for the latter years of this period the attitudinal decline was much less than for the earlier years. Indeed, for the period 1986 to 1996 'there has not been further deterioration in pupil attitude towards Christianity' (Kay and Francis 1996:43). The Church should not get too excited about this – there is no hint of revival here – but it does indicate that Christianity is unlikely to disappear entirely and that a committed core of people is always likely to remain. This committed core includes at least some of the 356,000 11 to 19 year olds in church on an average Sunday (Brierley 2006) and those who come to midweek activities. It includes the several thousand who attend annual youth events such as Soul Survivor and !Audacious for a week of worship, prayer, Bible study and social action; and the hundreds of British youth who go on pilgrimages to Lourdes, Taizé, Walsingham, Santiago de Compostella and other places. Indeed, for a minority of young people who engage with Christianity despite prevailing trends to do otherwise, religious faith may be *more* significant than it was for previous generations. Moreover, while many Christian affiliates do not go to church on a regular basis we cannot assume that their sense of belonging to Christianity means nothing to them. Here Grace Davie's concept of vicarious religion is important.

Vicarious religion

> The term [vicarious religion] has been coined in order to convey *the notion of religion performed by an active minority but on behalf of a much larger number, who (implicitly at least) not only understand, but, quite clearly, approve of what the minority is doing.* (Davie 2007a:22)

Davie suggests that while church attendance figures are falling, many people do still look to the Church for help at critical moments in their lives, particularly in relation to performing rites of passage. We have already discussed baptisms marking the birth of a child. Two-fifths of infants and children being baptized may be less than for previous generations, but it is still a lot of people. Around a third of weddings in England and Wales (ONS 2009a) and the majority of funerals still involve a Christian ceremony despite the fact that there are secular alternatives available for each of these occasions. While people increasingly want to personalise these occasional services and bring secular elements to them, Davie nevertheless observes that such innovation tends to take place within institutional structures. In other words, people still want the 'religious bit' to authenticate the ceremony (Barley 2006:13). What to do about death was one of the issues the young people in our study raised as being significant to them and is something we shall come back to in Chapter 3.

A second element of vicarious religion is that 'church leaders and churchgoers believe on behalf of others' (2007a:23). Here Davie points to the fact that whatever ideas people hold themselves, they still tend to be disconcerted when clergy appear not to be upholding Christian belief. She gives the example of the controversy around David Jenkins, the Church of England Archbishop of Durham (1984–1994), when he was portrayed in the press as challenging the truth of the Resurrection. More recently the current Archbishop of Canterbury, Rowan Williams, raised eyebrows when he suggested Britain might need to take account of Islamic Sharia law (BBC News 2008).

Third, vicarious religion means that 'church leaders and churchgoers are expected to embody moral codes on behalf of others' (2007a:23). When bishops or clergy fail to be the embodiment of propriety and compassion they are ridiculed, accused of hypocrisy and met with disappointment.

Finally, Davie suggests that religion may operate vicariously insofar as churches provide a 'space for the vicarious debate of unresolved issues in modern societies' (2007a:23). She quotes the media interest in the Anglican debate around homosexual priests as a case in point. Davie concludes that such 'public attention demands that we understand how religious institutions matter even to those who appear not to be "participants" in them' (2007a:25).

As we consider our conversations with young people we take up Davie's challenge to find out if and how Christianity matters to young people. In some ways it appears that our unchurched and dechurched young people did have something of a vicarious relationship with Christianity and the Church. Moreover, our sample of young people who strongly identified with the Christian faith and were regular churchgoers may well turn out to be part of the minority which sustains the faith for the wider population in the years to come.

Keeping the faith

As well as being interested in how young people relate to Christianity we are also interested in the social influences that young people feel help or hinder them in the development of their personal knowledge and understanding of the faith. In other words, what factors do young people experience as shaping their 'Christian consciousness'? This is a matter of faith transmission. In this respect we find the work of the French sociologist Danièle Hervieu-Léger and the American theologian Stanley Hauerwas helpful in our analysis of the views of the English young people who took part in our study. From each of their two disciplines, Hervieu-Léger and Hauerwas talk about the importance of community (past and present) and tradition for the appropriation, application and maintenance of faith and values. The faith community according to Hervieu-Léger (2000) provides a 'chain of memory' and for Hauerwas (1981:4a) embodies tradition and story. As we shall argue in later chapters, the chain of Christian memory for our young people is under severe strain since most are not part of faith communities. This makes the transmission of the Christian faith difficult (Chapter 4) which in turn has implications not just for what people believe, but for how they live their lives on the basis of their beliefs. Hauerwas, from his theological perspective, is clear in his view that people integrate the Christian faith into how they live their lives through the Church or not at all. This is a discussion we take up in Chapter 5 when we consider what difference religious beliefs make to young people in their day-to-day lives. Hauerwas' work also underpins the theological analysis we conduct in Chapter 7 in Part Two. For Part One we stick with sociology and Hervieu-Léger's concept of religion as a chain of memory.

Religion as a chain of memory

Hervieu-Léger (2000) draws attention to three characteristics of religion. These are not specific to Christianity, although her examples draw from the French experience of Roman Catholicism.[8]

Expression of believing

Religion, she suggests, involves the 'expression of believing' by which she means not just subscribing to a particular set of propositional beliefs, but rather active participation in the culture of faith – its convictions, stories, language, ritual etc. For the believer this provides a meaningful order to life, a sense of identity and purpose, hope for this world and the next. In other words, believing is an expression of faith which makes life ontologically secure and meaningful. 'Believing is belief in action, as it is experienced' (Hervieu-Léger 2000:72).

Community and heritage

Religion also involves a 'chain' or 'lineage of belief'. This means that religious believing is not a solitary act on the part of the individual but depends (even if very remotely) on a community which maintains the culture of faith, gives it stability and passes it on from one generation to the next. Put another way, although each believer has to appropriate and interpret a religious tradition for himself, he nevertheless needs to inherit something of the tradition in the first place. Even the solitary hermit is part of an historic tradition which has been sustained by a community past and present. Thus the present is understood through its relationship to the past, and the 'past contains the future' (Hervieu-Léger 2000:125). Communal as well as individual acts of recalling the past through the enactment of religious traditions keep belief alive by invoking its memory and locating present day life in an unfolding story that goes back centuries even transcending history.

Validating tradition

The 'chain of religious memory' not only gives religion stability and continuity but is also the basis of validating it: 'there is no religion without the authority of a tradition being invoked (whether explicitly, half-explicitly or implicitly) in support of the act of believing' (Hervieu-Léger 2000:76). The structure for the management and control of the memory varies for different groups. As Hervieu-Léger explains:

> The controlled mobilization of memory by a priesthood who are so ordained by a religious establishment differs from the charismatic mobilization of memory initiated by a prophet. But in all instances it is the recognized ability to expound the true memory of the group that constitutes the core of religious power (2000:126).

The difficulty for the Church is that the processes of Western modernization undermine the authority of tradition, fragment community and threaten the plausibility and relevance of beliefs which give expression to Christian faith. The chain of Christian memory, which the Church once managed, is therefore dissipated and eroded.

That said, for Hervieu-Léger the religious inclination itself does not go away. People still need a basis on which to make sense of their lives, work out how to live together, maintain hope in the face of difficulties, interpret death and so on. In other words, people still need to put faith in something whether articulated through an alternative religion, a political system, science, or as Karen says in our opening paragraph, simply having faith in their self. Consequently modernization potentially opens up opportunities for the reorganization of faith, the emergence of 'new' beliefs and the introduction of different memories; whilst the Church is left with the task of trying to preserve what remains of the Christian memory so that it does not disappear altogether. We can see the difficulties of the task if we look more closely at the process of modernization and the legacy it has left in terms of rationalization, pluralism and individualization. We will see in the rest of this book the impact these have had on the transmission of faith and young people's (dis)inclination and capacity to engage with Christianity today.

Modernization and the collapse of memory

The term 'modernization' embraces a range of processes that reorganized society from traditional agrarian based communities to modern industrial nations.[9] Early modern societies were relatively stable local communities. Individuals knew their role in life since it was largely prescribed by tradition and normative control. There was no separation of public and private realms as we know them today, and consequently individuals could be known as 'total persons' (Wilson 1982) – those who worked together also played and lived together. As a result of this organization, kinship loyalties were strong, not least because family members depended upon one another for their day-to-day existence. Family therefore provided the main mechanism by which social ties were stabilised across time and space (Giddens 1991:102). Church overlay this social order. Families were incorporated into a community through their location in a parish, and this had historic continuity. 'For centuries,' Hervieu-Léger writes, 'the parish represented *the* society of memory' (2000:132). The village church and cemetery gave testimony to the gathered community past and present. Church provided a means whereby the common life shared within the local community could be celebrated, regulated and understood in relation to a cosmic order. It gave people a 'providential interpretation to life and nature' (Giddens 1991:102). In short, in early modern society kinship relations, local community, belief and tradition all came together to create an environment which established and maintained the Christian faith, and provided a coherent way of living that could be passed on from one generation to the next through the social fabric of day-to-day life.

As modernization advanced all this changed. Belief became disembedded from social life as communities were fragmented and the traditional authority held by the Church for validating belief was gradually transferred to individuals and the new 'priests' of science and bureaucracy. The chain of memory then became harder to sustain. Three processes which contributed to difficulties for sustaining memory and which held a legacy discernible amongst our young people are rationalization, pluralization and individualization.

Rationalization

Rationalization as part of the 'project of modernity' is concerned with the development of human autonomy and progress based on reason, scientific enquiry, technological advance and means-ends utility. Science and technology can undermine religious believing. This is not so much because they question the adequacy of religious thinking for understanding the world, since although they may do this, people usually find ways to protect themselves from the destruction of cherished beliefs (Bruce 2001:253–255). Rather, it is because science and technology have very successfully allowed human beings to take control of the world, subdue it, innovate and make improvements for living so that most people today look for rational explanations of the world and rational solutions to problems, thereby sidelining God and religion. Berger et al. (1974) refer to this as the development of a collective 'technological consciousness'. Thus, when sick most people in the first instance look to medicine for a cure rather than to prayer; the latter may accompany or follow but it is not the first point of reference for the modern mind.

Furthermore, science and technology are always advancing. Scientific paradigms are expected to change as knowledge develops. There is little room for tradition here. Similarly, modern societies aim to be as well organized and efficient as possible in the performance and administration of public life. If traditional ways of doing things fall short of the mark they are replaced by a more rational approach. This sometimes backfires of course. Bureaucracies, for example, may start out trying to be rational and efficient but end up obfuscating and complicating things. Improvements to the system are then sought but nobody suggests going back to tradition; the modern world is just too complicated for that.

For young people growing up in the early part of the 21st century, scientific and technological development continues apace, especially in relation to mass media and electronic communications. This has further flattened tradition. In an age of rapid information flows and instantaneous images it is difficult to maintain a sense of continuity and connection between events. Hervieu-Léger argues that the perennial airing of concerns over young people's lack of religious and cultural knowledge is often misplaced. It is not that young people lack information, since there is plenty of that available to them via the media and internet.

> What is at issue is whether young people have the ability to organize this mass of information by relating it to a lineage to which they spontaneously see themselves as belonging (2000:129-30).

For many it seems that they do not.

Pluralism and religious diversity

Another feature of modernization is religious diversity. Christianity has always contained multiple traditions brought about by schism and innovation, but modernity extends the range of religious beliefs beyond Christianity in Western Europe, not least because the development of transport and communications technologies has contributed, among other things, to the global availability of ideas and beliefs.

Geographical mobility gets easier as modernity progresses. As travel becomes faster, safer and more affordable so people from different cultures mix and religious diversity becomes an increasingly salient aspect of life. In the late modern[10] period migration has increased the number of people in Britain belonging to non-Christian faiths. These numbers are boosted by higher fertility rates among non-White populations, making for a younger age profile amongst non-Christian religious populations. For example, a third of Muslims in Britain are under 16 years of age, and just over a third are aged between 16 and 34, whereas just under one fifth of the Christian population is under 16 and just over one fifth falls into the 16 to 34 age bracket (ONS 2004a).

The perception of the extent of diversity sometimes outweighs the reality of numbers, however. According to the 2006 British Social Attitude Survey 3.3% of adults identify themselves as belonging to Islam, 1.4% to Hinduism, 0.5% to Judaism, 0.2% to Sikhism and 0.2% identify themselves as Buddhists, which compares to 47% belonging to Christianity (Park et al. 2008). For the largest minority group, this gives a total Muslim population in Britain of around 1.6 million compared to 41 million Christians (ONS 2004b).[11] The profile is more mixed for 18 to 24 year olds, but still in favour of Christianity – 27% Christian compared to 14% other world faiths. It is also worth bearing in mind that some geographical areas, such as London, the Midlands and north-west, are far more religiously diverse than other areas; religious pluralism is therefore more apparent in some areas than others.

Another source of religious diversity comes from the emergence of new types of spiritualities which are separate from mainstream institutional religions and which focus on the interior life of individuals – 'new age' spiritualities or spiritualities of the 'holistic milieu' like reiki, transcendental meditation and yoga (Heelas and Woodhead 2005). In addition, there are alternative spiritualities such as paganism, as well as a whole range of folk beliefs and practices (astrology, fortune-telling and the like) which have always existed alongside the institutional church in Britain.

On a societal level the jury is out regarding the effect of diversity on the long-term maintenance of religious belief in general. It is sometimes argued that societies which enable religious and spiritual diversity to develop unencumbered thereby encourage religiosity and spirituality to flourish since people's different needs are catered for in a broad 'spiritual market'. The United States is usually given as an example of this. In Europe, however, where churches have tended to hold a religious monopoly over large populations, pluralism is potentially more problematic for religious belief since it means that faith can no longer be taken for granted as it once could be and people have to choose. Under these circumstances a varied spiritual market holds the potential for relativism and a loss of religious plausibility. Since different religions hold different views, so the logic goes, they cannot all be right so maybe none of them are and all are rejected. Even if an individual is convinced of her own faith position, social harmony requires tolerance and accommodation of other people's different faith positions. In the end some may suggest this may mean ignoring all religions equally so that none is given priority. Either way pluralism can potentially sideline religion.

In our analysis of young people's engagement with Christianity we were interested in the extent to which they explored the spiritual marketplace more generally and whether diversity was a barrier or motivation to faith. As we shall see in Chapters 3 and 4 the answer for our young people was that the spiritual marketplace neither stimulated nor hindered the religious inclination in any obvious way. Moreover, for our young people there was relatively little evidence of 'pick-and-mix' spirituality – i.e. the selection of beliefs and practices from a range of different religious traditions to form a unique individual cosmology – it was more a case of religious 'make-do and mend'. We explain in Chapter 3.

Individualization

Another important feature of modernization is the rise of individualism which runs alongside the fragmentation of local communities. As early modernity advanced and people left their rural homes for work in the newly emerging urban industrial centres, so traditional communities fragmented and the public world of work became separated from the private world of family and home life. Functional rationality meant that spheres of social organization became increasingly specialized and subject to secular rules of efficiency and progress. Gradually the Church's social influence diminished and became subject to secular control. Indeed, one of the reasons we were interested in young people's experience of Christian youth work in the current research was because we wanted to know whether the professionalization of this provision on the grounds of secular qualifications and regulation affected its mission orientation.

Social differentiation increases in the modern world as new areas of expert knowledge develop and advance in the public realm. Late modernity, however, is also characterized by the fragmentation of the private realm. In the post-War period attitudes and values around relationships and personal morality have become more liberal. One aspect of this is the fragmentation and instability of family life, which can be problematic for young people developing a sense of communal belonging and lineage that forms part of identity. Hervieu-Léger goes so far as to suggest this may be central to young people's lack of engagement with religion:

> The collapse of the traditional family, wholly dedicated to biological reproduction and the transmission of a biological, material and symbolic inheritance from generation to generation, probably counts as a central factor in the disintegration of the imagined continuity that lies at the heart of the modern crisis of religion (2000:133).

Hervieu-Léger takes the growing interest in family history in France as evidence that people are trying to repair their sense of lineage and community. The same trend is apparent in Britain. Television programmes such as *Who Do You Think You Are?* have become popular, at least among older people. The heritage industry is also big business. Interestingly the Church seems to benefit from this in some respects since visits to cathedrals have risen over the last few years. More generally, however, Hervieu-Léger points to the development of 'elective fraternities' which serve to fill the void left by family fragmentation.

> [In an elective fraternity it] is not recognition of common ancestry that determines the relationship between brothers, but the experience of brotherhood justifying the invention of common ancestry. An elective fraternity corresponds to a certain community of values and references which has developed through shared interests, experience and hardships. Elective fraternity is a relationship that is both willed and ideal in the sense that it is presumed to bring into being what ties of blood are so often incapable of ensuring between members of a family – real solidarity, transparency of thought and communication, and common values and memories (2000:150).

It is not difficult to regard youth gangs as one type of example of an 'elective fraternity', but any group – and indeed multiple groups – could fit the bill. The importance of family (fragmented or not) and friends to young people was such a dominant feature to emerge in our research that it is a point we come back to in our discussion in later chapters.

The fragmention of family reflects wider social trends towards individualism and subjectivity in late modern society. There is today a 'compulsion to individualism' (Beck and Beck-Gernsheim 2002). Young people are charged with the responsibility of finding their own way through life in an increasingly uncertain world utilizing whatever cultural resources they can access. Religions are cultural resources which young people may – or may not – choose to draw upon as they work out their identity and lifestyle, but they are treated more as objects of consumption than obligation (Davie 2007b:96–98). In this respect, the construction of selfhood has become something of a 'reflexive project' (Giddens 1991). Under these circumstances it is personal authenticity rather than role or duty that comes with tradition, that becomes an important guiding principle for establishing who one is in the world. To move away from religion for just a moment, one has only to think of the different pathways that young people might take in their transition from youth to adulthood to see the range of choices they are required to make; far more than their parents or grandparents had to consider in their youth. Young people today are likely to have a say in which school they want to go to, what courses they wish to follow and which exams to take. On leaving school they may take up vocational courses, have a gap year, enter further education, go straight into employment, or if unsuccessful in any of these may find themselves as a 'NEET' – not in employment, education or training. From here other trajectories follow which are neither necessarily linear nor permanent. Young people may go to college or university after a period of work or unemployment. Higher education does not guarantee employment, further training may be needed and unemployment may still beckon. In the workplace young people do not expect to follow in their parents' footsteps, nor do they expect to have a 'job for life'. Whether it is making the best of the situation they find themselves in or engaging in specific forward-looking life planning, young people have to choose.

Similarly in matters of relationships by the time young people come to choose partners (gay or straight), they may have already negotiated the complexities of parental divorce and managed a range of 'blended family' relationships over the short or longer term. A young person may leave home for a while and cohabit with a partner, then return to the parental household/s. They may marry (or not) after having children rather than before; they may divorce and enter into serial relationships. The point is that there is no longer a normative trajectory of education, employment, heterosexual marriage, setting up a home and having children. Deviations from this pattern are expected and carry little or no stigma – it is all down to the individual.

Depending on how you look at it, young people live in exciting or stressful times – or both! For those with the resources and resourcefulness to cope with such freedoms life is good; for those without, life can be very difficult indeed and freedom can take its toll on a young person's wellbeing. Mørch and Andersen list the range of competencies young people need to engage fully in the project of self-construction imposed upon them: 'self-identity, reflexivity, self-assurance, knowledgeability, participation, individual basic trust in the world and one's self' (2006:71). It goes without saying that some young people are better placed than others regarding these competencies, and in this respect it is worth noting that individualization is not so complete that the limitations placed on access to resources by social class, gender and ethnicity have disappeared.

Happy midi-narrative revisited

We have discussed elsewhere the implicit worldview that young people utilize in everyday life when they engage with popular art and culture, capturing something of the freedom and responsibility they face when making sense of their lives (Savage et al 2006).[12] We called this the 'happy midi-narrative' – its structure runs something like this:

> My aim to be happy will be realized through me being myself, and connecting to others and the universe (without harming them). As I do this, I will create a meaningful and happy life. If we all make this individual effort (everyone's own responsibility), each person's happiness will sum into a corporate experience of unity and enjoyment. This happiness is meaningful in itself; it is the Ideal.

> [However] Bad things can happen in real life that prevent us from attaining this happiness: broken relationships, suffering, loneliness, depression, self-rejection, addiction, injustice, ageing. But each one of us is surrounded by resources of family and close friends who love us unconditionally. The popular arts [and popular culture] provide us with valuable resources: information, choice, creativity. With these, we can experience movement from the Actual (real life where bad things can happen) towards the Ideal (happiness).

> Having received help, having 'grown' as a result of the meaningful microcosm of family, friends and the popular arts, the happy Ideal that once eluded us is now possible. (Savage et al. 2006:39)

The assumption embedded in this worldview is that the meaningful happy Ideal is achievable. If it turns out that it is not then the disparity between expectation and reality can be very difficult to deal with. Once happiness is seen as a possibility it becomes an individual's responsibility to achieve it, and if it is not realized it is seen as nobody's fault but their own.

In terms of faith, the Happy midi-narrative is a secular worldview where the meaningful Ideal is achieved through individual resourcefulness (making use of the popular arts and culture), family and friends not through religious fulfilment. It is in these – family, friends and self – that young people put their trust and find hope for their future. We can call this 'immanent faith' – it is a 'this-worldly' faith. If immanent faith was implicit in our previous research, in the current study it is far more explicit. A further question then presents itself, namely, what is the relationship between immanent faith and Christianity? We take this up in Chapter 3.

The search for the happy Ideal should not be taken to suggest that young people are hedonistic and amoral. Happiness is relational and requires that others are not harmed. This point is echoed by Beck and Beck-Gernsheim (2002) who are keen to point out that while individualization focuses on subjectivity it does not mean that young people are necessarily selfish. They dismisses the epitaph that is sometimes applied to individualistic young people – the 'me generation' – as derogatory. They hold a rather more positive view and argue that young people adopt an ethical approach to life that embraces and respects the individuality of others as well as oneself. They refer to this as 'altruistic individualism': 'Thinking of oneself and living for others' (2002:28). In this respect Beck and Beck-Gernsheim are similar to Taylor (1991) who writes that individualism as a moral principle must offer some view on how the individual should live with others in society. Authenticity and dependence on others are not mutually exclusive.

As we shall see in Chapter 5, we found our young people are ethically minded and had a coherent, confident yet also conventional way of looking at the world in terms of purpose and moral living.

Possible futures

Given the difficulties modernity presents for traditional institutional religion it is not hard to understand why the Christian memory is fading from society. However, the circumstances of freedom and uncertainty that late modernity brings to the fore potentially offer some scope for religion – Christianity included – to re-emerge as a resource through which young people may establish a sense of identity and communal belonging. This does not, of course, mean a return to pre- or early modern society but a renegotiation of tradition to fit the late modern demand for authenticity and the perennial need for faith in something. As we listen to the young people in the rest of Part One and explore their differing views we get a sense of aspects of these possibilities coming through in subtle and nuanced ways. It is undoubtedly the case that the Christian memory is very faint and in many respects Generation Y are a largely unstoried or memoryless generation. On the other hand this offers unexpected opportunities for mission and for the Church to present itself and its traditions in its own authentic ways. We take up this theological discussion in Part Two.

2

Mission and method

In the previous chapter we set out the broad conceptual framework of our research into young people's faith and their relationship to Christianity. Here we locate it within the field of Christian youth work which gave rise to the initial study, and give an overview of the methodology we used. Our interest in Christian youth work is threefold. The first is a concern for the discipline itself. The second is that Christian youth work often acts as a microcosm for what happens in church and society. The third is that what happens in Christian youth work can be a forerunner for what happens later on in the Church.

History of youth work

Historically there is a long tradition of Christian involvement with children and young people in both education and mission. Ward (1996) believes that youth work as we understand it is a 19th-century invention and Breen (1993) argues that Christians have been significant in pioneering the main approaches to youth work we see today. The Sunday School movement, which started in the 18th century, had set a precedent for separate religious instruction for children, and Christian organizations such as the YMCA (1844) and the Boys' Brigade (1883) emerged in the 19th century to continue this educational work but with a clear evangelical focus. There was a realization that new ways of transmitting the Christian story needed to emerge to keep its memory alive. This was encapsulated by an Act of Parliament that allowed the Church of England to run special services outside of those previously authorized, and in response to this the Children's Special Service Mission (CSSM) was formed in 1867 and services specifically for children began to be held (Pollock 1959). This is one of the early examples of an organization emerging that established a tradition of transmitting the Christian story in a specific way linked into a specific set of beliefs about the Bible and faith.

CSSM is now Scripture Union and has the mission statement 'Using the Bible to inspire children, young people and adults to know God'.[1] It could be argued that Scripture Union has established a 'chain of memory' through its beach missions, holiday clubs and regular youth groups that for generations of children and young people have functioned as church without them necessarily connecting with an institutional Church. The same could be said for a range of parachurch organizations such as Youth for Christ and Urban Saints who provide activities for young people with a clear evangelical agenda of transmitting the story of faith to those who do not know it.

Alongside youth work as evangelism came the development of welfare organizations such as that of Dr Barnardo, who opened his first home in 1867. Arguably, then, Christian work with children and young people encompassed education, mission and social action, although for many mission was the driving force, particularly among evangelicals. This focus on mission is reflected in background Christian youth work texts that have shaped the context for the youth workers who took part in our project. Ashton (1986), for example, claims that the 'first aim of Christian youth work must be to present a young person with the claims of Jesus Christ'. *Youth A Part*, a major Church of England report, makes clear in its theology chapter that 'Youth work needs to be understood as a dimension of the Church's mission' (Church of England 1996). One of the most influential books which still shapes perceptions of youth work is Pete Ward's (1997) *Youthwork and the Mission of God* where he elaborates his concepts of 'inside out' and 'outside in'. 'Inside out' involves working with churched young people out to those on the fringe of the Church, while 'outside in' involves working with the unchurched and looks at drawing them towards and inside the Church.

The youth work we researched tended to be 'outside in' and would often use more of an informal education methodology than that of overt evangelism. Informal education is

> a reflective exercise which enables young people to learn from their experience, develop their capacity to think critically and engage in 'sense-making' as a process of continuous self discovery and re-creation (Young 1999).

Informal education has as its primary focus a young person's relationship with herself and society whereas in a missional approach the core concern is a young person's relationship with God. We found that youth workers tended to concentrate on the former. Attempts to raise Christian consciousness, such as might be considered integral to a Christian missional approach, ended up as quite subtle and often completely missed by the young people. The hope was that the young people would ask questions of the youth worker's faith. The reality of a memoryless generation was that for the majority of young people this would rarely happen, if at all.

The discipline of Christian youth work

Christian youth work as a profession has had a rapid growth. While a definitive figure is hard to come by, one recent estimate suggests that there are around 8000 youth workers employed through churches in the UK.[2] We have been involved to different degrees in the training and delivery of youth work and so we have an interest in its continuing development. In 1995 we helped to pioneer the development of the Centre for Youth Ministry (CYM),[3] offering both a theology degree and a professional youth work qualification in the same package. We were therefore interested in exploring whether or not this professionalized approach to youth work had tempered the more missional approach that historically has been prevalent in evangelicalism – the tradition of the majority of the projects researched. We will offer some answers to this question throughout the book and here explore some of the background.

Ward argues that the increase in the numbers of churches employing youth workers predates the growth in degree level Christian youth work courses. He says that the trend started as evangelical churches responded to parents wanting their children to be nurtured in a safe environment, safety being what he believes to be the hidden agenda of evangelical youth work (1996:184). Many of these churches could mobilize the funds needed to employ someone and 'suddenly money and an emotionally charged agenda are being drawn together and the result has been the development of full-time youth ministry in this country' (Ward 1996:184). In other words, in an increasingly secular society Christian parents wanted their children to join their tradition and become part of the same chain of memory. The increasing number of jobs that became available for youth workers helped to spawn a variety of training opportunities. These largely fall into two categories; Christian value based professionally qualifying courses where theology is studied alongside youth and community work (and graduates are qualified to work in the statutory or voluntary sectors), and theology degrees with a youth work element. These two possibilities are indicative of one of the ongoing debates between youth work employees and employers. This has been identified as the difference between youth work and youth ministry. Youth work is seen more broadly as educative, not overtly Christian, community focused and with a mission agenda at the social action end of the spectrum. Youth ministry is work with young people who are already part of the Church and incorporates evangelism and discipleship. In the terms of our study youth ministers are those who are explicitly committed to enabling young people to engage with Christianity's 'chain of memory' as a part of an authentic storied community. Youth workers on the other hand are working in a community-focused setting (rather than overtly church or discipleship-focused ministry) and have to balance their passion for mission with their desire to take seriously the professional values of being educative, participative, empowering and committed to equal opportunities (Davies 1999).

This divide between youth work and youth ministry is discussed by Brierley (2003) who argues that rather than being an 'either/or', it should be a 'both/ and'. He sees youth work as the broad discipline incorporating all those who are engaged in informal education and suggests that youth ministry should be seen as a specialism within this broader field. He acknowledges that there was a breakdown in the partnership between Church and state where 'the statutory sector labelled youth ministry as unprofessional and proselytising and the Church responded with the claim that youth work was devoid of spiritual significance' (Brierley 2003:57). There are still residues of these stereotypes around and this can influence youth work provision, funding opportunities, and self and external perception of the youth workers and the activities they provide. On the other hand there are some encouraging signs too. The National Youth Agency (the body that co-ordinates the validation of professionally qualifying courses) has published a book on spirituality and spiritual development for youth work as well as a book of activities designed to enhance and encourage spirituality (Green 2006). There is also a growing acknowledgement of the role of spirituality in people's lives and the importance that this has for those in the caring professions. Moss, for example, argues that for a practitioner to ignore the spiritual dimension of their own or their client's selfhood is to fail to meet 'the demands of best practice, and is not likely to be able to offer anything like the holistic service to which people are entitled' (2005:14). Projects such as Church of England and Oasis UK Academies show how Christian organizations are also getting involved in delivering mainstream services.[4]

The projects that we researched are involved in Christian community based youth work rather than youth ministry. Their focus is on young people outside of the Church and in general their approach is one of informal education. The consequence of this has perhaps been to reduce the amount of overt evangelism that takes place in community focused youth work run by Christians which may mean that what was offered was little different to other providers. If this were to be so then questions may need to be asked as to why the Church invests in such work. This exchange from one of our interviews would be typical of the move away from overt attempts to raise Christian consciousness in a community based club:

Interviewer: You said that when you were younger there was like the 'epilogue' bit.

Karen: That was fine because it was like, they would do a play of it. They would take a story out of the Bible and do a play and it was really good, but they stopped doing it.

Interviewer: Why did they stop doing it?

Karen: I think because some people, you know, they don't really like, you know, when it comes to reading the Bible, I don't think they like it at all. They just wasn't interested, so they don't really like it.

Interviewer: So how long ago was that?

Karen: Oh years, well

Interviewer: Ten years, twelve years?

Karen: About, I think nearly like 13, . . .

Interviewer: Oh OK, a while back.

There is still an uneasiness between the successors of the youth work/youth ministry debate. In our experience of training youth workers there can be some mutual scepticism in this debate with those who style their work as 'detached' or 'incarnational' seeing themselves as doing 'real' youth work and those who are doing what might be seen as the soft option of youth ministry working with churched middle class young people. However, to call itself 'Christian' youth work at some point needs to explore the idea of transmission of the Christian story past and present and how young people are being drawn into the Christian community.

Youth work as a microcosm of Church and Society

In its current guise as a deliverer of a professional youth work qualification, Christian youth work training is engaging directly with the interaction between a Christian narrative and the ethics of secular liberalism. Good youth work from a statutory standpoint

- Offers quality support to young people which helps them achieve and progress;
- Enables young people to have their voice heard and influence decision making at various levels;
- Provides a diversity of personal and social development opportunities;
- Promotes intervention and prevention to address individual, institutional and policy causes of disaffection and exclusion;
- Is well planned, focusing on achieving outcomes that meet young people's needs and priorities (National Youth Agency 2007:7).

Far from making any claim about faith transmission, statutory youth work is more likely to be hostile towards any form of religious propagation. Our interest is in how this secular agenda has affected Christian youth work's attempts to raise a Christian consciousness.

Another way in which youth work acts as a microcosm of the wider issues facing the Church and society is in the interface between young people's self perception and how they are portrayed in the media. What is reflected back to young people about themselves from the mass media is not always encouraging. A Google search for the phrase 'demonized young people' scored 152,000 hits.[5] The international edition of *Time* magazine for April 2008 had on its cover a young man in a hoodie in the centre of a stylized Union Jack with the headline 'Unhappy, Unloved and Out of Control – An epidemic of violence, crime and drunkenness has made Britain scared of its young'.

A major concern for youth workers is how the media might affect young people's perception of themselves. IPPR North undertook a day consultation in Sunderland and found that young people were concerned about media perceptions of their generation. One young man commented that: 'The media very much feeds stigma. They paint a very unfair picture of young people' (Sweeney 2008). What is perhaps more concerning is that the researchers found that young people felt disconnected from society and that adults such as shopkeepers, bus drivers and the police had negative views of them and that some adults were verbally abusive and threatening. Youth workers agreed that young people did not feel part of their local community.

A research project by the National Children's Bureau found that negative media portrayals can affect young people's self-perception and their behaviour, influencing such things as where they could go with friends and how they dressed. It also contributes to young people themselves being afraid of other young people whom they do not know (Clark et al. 2008). In seeing how young people are treated and what impact this has on them we can see some of the wider issues in building community cohesion and positive identities. Christian youth work has an honourable role in enhancing young people's sense of self regard and wellbeing. The Frontier Youth Trust Campaign 'Labels R4 Jars Not Young People' was an attempt to address such issues.[6] In such ways Christian youth workers seek to challenge the dominant media narrative about young people and replace it with one which is more in keeping with a Christian narrative that is based on the worth and value of all humanity made in the image of God.

Youth work as a forerunner of trends

The third reason for our interest is that an early exposure to changing cultural trends means that youth work can act as a forerunner for what then happens in the wider Church. The youth work constituency has more room than the wider Church to experiment and so it is not unusual to have a situation of youth-work-today-church-tomorrow. This has been most recently illustrated by the guidelines for training pioneer ministers in the Church of England. These guidelines were agreed by the House of Bishops in January 2006 and mirror the mixed mode model of training evident in the youth work constituency,[7] with students working in churches and travelling to dispersed campuses for module teaching. The experience both in this type of training and in working with Generation Y young people gives us room to reflect back to the wider Church some of the lessons learned and insights gained. We do this in Chapter 7 looking at how the 'Fresh Expressions' initiative might engage with Generation Y.

One of our findings is that young people are looking for authenticity. Theirs is a generation growing up in a culture where identity is regularly contested and the exploration of faith identity has to be countered with a militant atheism being regularly propagated in parts of the liberal media. This means that part of the role of youth workers is to help young people explore who they are within the context of this debate. The only way that this can be done is to help young people understand the story and tradition of which they are a part, and to help them develop a community-focused (as opposed to individual) identity that locates who they are in relation to the Christian narrative as lived out by others. Dean, in *Practicing Passion* (2004), talks about helping young people find a cause worth dying for. She offers a theologically rooted approach to youth ministry that contrasts with sociological and psychological methods. She argues that young people are passionate and we need to connect to their passions. To do this youth workers need to be passionate themselves with a willingness to be up front about their faith and what impact this has on the rest of their lives. In this way youth workers can lead the way in being distinctively Christian and overt in their faith.

A cultural trend that has particularly influenced Generation Y is the growth, diversity and availability of technology for communication. Today's young people have grown up using computers, have never known a world without mobile phones and are adept at adapting and using technology for education, friendship and information gathering. Youth workers communicate regularly through text messages, do pastoral care on *Facebook* and have the capacity within their youth group to produce multi-media and multi-sensory worship and learning activities. Thus youth workers communicate with young people in the same way that young people communicate with their friends. This is perhaps something for the wider Church to learn from. It still appears to be a small number of churches that make best use of the media available to them to connect with their congregations other than on Sundays. Virtual community building is commonplace in youth work and often young people will feel more comfortable in this environment. There are, however, safeguarding issues arising from the use of e-communications and the lower levels of inhibition about disclosure in the virtual setting that need to be considered when working in this sphere.

Indeed, awareness of people's vulnerabilities and the need to adopt practices which minimize risk is becoming an increasingly salient aspect of ministry. Generation Y are the first generation to go through church youth work when child protection and safeguarding policies have been required and implemented. For many youth workers, both professional and voluntary, there is a greater understanding of appropriate boundaries and the importance of respect and empowering young people to make decisions for themselves and a greater awareness of the potential for abuse in more subtle ways than physical or sexual. However, this can lead to risk aversion and a reluctance to follow what could be Holy Spirit-inspired impulses because of the dangers of breaking the rules and facing disciplinary action. While we are in no way advocating that youth workers behave in such a way as to put young people or themselves in danger, some of the ways in which young people have been integrated into the faith community in the past are less available to them today because of limits on hospitality, for example, that some church youth work policies impose. Interestingly, there seems to be much less overt guidance on ministry among adults, although this is beginning to change with published guidelines such as *Promoting a Safe Church* (Church of England 2006). At their best these provide helpful boundaries and guidance and at their worst they help to develop a culture of suspicion and mistrust. In this way some of the dilemmas and issues faced by youth workers will increasingly be felt by those who minister to adults.

The story of our research

In order to address our research interests we adopted a method that would allow us to get as detailed a picture of the young people's experience of Christian youth work as possible. We therefore decided that while we would include some summary statistics for descriptive clarification, our main approach would be qualitative. Qualitative methods are traditionally used by social researchers to consider the construction of meaning and experience. The idea is to elicit rich, nuanced data which gives voice to participants, in our case young people.

We used our Christian youth work contacts to build up a sample of participating projects across England. We do not claim that these projects, or the young people attending them, are necessarily statistically representative of Christian youth work or young people country-wide. This was not our intention. Rather, we adopted a sampling strategy that would provide an extended case study and give us a useful critical context in which to address our research interests. We collected data to 'saturation point', which means we got to the stage when new data was simply repeating information we had collected earlier in the study. We are therefore confident that our findings are robust. Projects were chosen from 31 locations across the country – some based in villages, others in towns, suburbs or urban areas – that had a community focus (we were less interested in youth work aimed only at young churchgoers, such as Sunday Schools). The projects each had a mission-oriented sponsoring organization and a team of professional staff who were sympathetic to the sponsor's aims.[8] We would in theory expect projects with these characteristics to have at least some effect on young people's Christian consciousness.

We defined Christian consciousness as young people's knowledge and under-standing of Christianity as a publicly available religious and moral worldview, and an awareness of Christianity in relation to young people's own sense of personal spirituality, religious identity and faith. (The latter could, of course, equally mean a young person developing an awareness that Christianity is *not* a part of their spirituality, identity and faith or a recognition that it is.) We then developed this idea to look at the social influences on the transmission of Christian faith.

Data was gathered in two phases. The first involved structured questionnaires and semi-structured interviews undertaken by ourselves. These were designed to gain a detailed picture of young people's religious identities, beliefs and values, their experiences of Christian youth work and whether or not it had helped them to explore Christian faith or religious ideas. We received 297 completed questionnaires and conducted interviews with 107 young people. These encompassed both young people who attended church on Sundays as well as the midweek youth and community project and those who did not. We distinguish between 'frequent churchgoers' who go to church at least once a month and 'infrequent churchgoers' who rarely (less than once a month) or never go to church. The infrequent churchgoers were largely unchurched or dechurched young people whose contact with church services was restricted to school services, Christmas and family occasions such as baptisms, weddings and funerals. (Table 2.1 gives details of the young people who took part in Phase 1.)

The number of frequent churchgoers answering our questionnaire (54%) is high relative to the infrequent churchgoers (46%) given the figures on youth churchgoing nationally (see Chapter 1). We have already noted that our method was not geared at securing a nationally representative sample; nevertheless, the high rate of church attendance is intriguing and needs to be considered. It may be that Christian youth groups disproportionately attract Christian young people even when they are aimed at the whole local community. In the 2005 English Church Census Brierley (2006:218) notes that approximately 45% of young people who attended church-run mid-week activities were also Sunday churchgoers, leaving 55% who were not. He makes the point that this still means that these youth activities enable the Church to retain contact with around 181,000 young people it otherwise would have no contact with; and in particular with the 11 to 14 age range. This is significant because the early teen years are when young people tend to make their own decision about continued church contact. In our study, however, a more likely explanation of the high proportion of frequent churchgoers is that churchgoing young people are more willing to answer a questionnaire about Christianity than those who do not go

Table 2.1 Characteristics of young people in Phase 1

Questionnaire respondents

Age:	11–13 years = 40%. 14–15 years = 33%. 16–18 years = 26%. 19–23 years = 1%
Gender:	Male = 42%. Female = 58%.
Ethnicity:	White = 95%. Black = 2%. Asian = 1%. Dual Heritage = 2%.
Religious Identity:	Church of England = 42%. Roman Catholic = 3.5%. Other Christian = 27%. Agnostic = 10%. Atheist = 4.5%. Don't Know = 13%.
Church attendance:	Frequents = 54%. Infrequents = 46%.

Interview participants

Age:	8–10 years = 4%. 11–13 years = 17%. 14–15 years = 45%. 16–23 years = 34%.
Gender:	Male = 54%. Female = 46%.
Ethnicity:	White = 72%. Black = 17%. Asian = 1%. Dual Heritage = 10%.
Church attendance:	Frequents = 23%. Infrequents = 77%.

Table 2.2 Characteristics of infrequent church going young people in Phase 2

Age:	11–13 years = 15%. 14–15 years = 25%. 16–23 years = 60%.
Gender:	Male = 51%. Female = 49%.
Ethnicity:	White = 70%. Black = 13%. Dual Heritage = 17%.
Church attendance:	Infrequents = 100%.

to church. As we shall see in later chapters, many young people simply are not that interested in giving religion much thought and are therefore not inclined to give up valuable time socializing with friends to fill out a questionnaire on it. The young people's participation in our study was entirely voluntary and we did not press them to fill in the questionnaire if they did not want to do so. The questionnaire sample we did secure, however, had enough of both infrequent and frequent churchgoers to allow us to compare the experiences of the two groups. This turned out to be very useful since there were important differences between them. For the interviews in Phase 1 infrequent churchgoers were the majority group.

The second phase used youth workers as practitioner researchers to explore the impact of an intervention designed to raise Christian consciousness using a research tool to establish young people's perspectives on six topic areas – spirituality, purpose of life, prayer, belief in God, decision-making and Christianity. We asked the youth workers to identify up to six young people who were largely unchurched to take part in this phase. We worked with 13 youth workers and 44 young people completed this phase. (Table 2.2 gives details of the young people who took part in Phase 2.)

For their analysis, the research team used a grounded thematic approach which involved looking for themes and issues that emerged from the data. The qualitative data analysis software programme *N6* helped us to be systematic in our approach to the large dataset. As we wrote up the research we individually and collectively presented conference papers and wrote articles on such topics as place, prayer and family as part of a critical dialogue with the wider field which helped in the process of exploring and refining our ideas. Finally in November 2008 we presented the findings from the empirical phase to the youth workers we had worked with to test our conclusions with them. All through the project we also had an advisory panel with practitioner and theological expertise who were able to guide and support us.

The next three chapters present our findings. All the names of the young people and youth workers have been anonymized with pseudonyms to protect their identity.

3

Bedroom spirituality

We saw in Chapter 1 that late modern society is not conducive to the maintenance of the Christian faith as expressed through the historic church traditions. Rationalization tends to sideline it, pluralism makes it a matter of choice, individualization disembeds faith from the community and subjectivizes belief and practice. We therefore address two questions in this chapter. First, in what do late modern young people believe and trust which gives them a sense of ontological security or, to put it more simply, a basic sense that they are 'OK'? Second, in what practical ways if any does the cultural Christian memory inform whatever constellation of faith young people have? In this respect we are particularly interested in youth who are not frequent churchgoers.

On the basis of our research here and elsewhere (Collins 1997, Savage et al. 2006), we suggest that faith is dynamic with multiple points of reference, the most significant of which are the 'secular trinity' of family, friends and the reflexive self. For many of our young people everyday meaning, hope, purpose and ultimately happiness were to be derived from good and trustworthy relationships with family and friends, and from the exercise and expression of authentic reflexive selfhood. As such their faith was this-worldly and 'immanent'. Immanent faith was usually good enough to sustain young people's 'courage to be' (Tillich 1962) from day to day – usually, but not always. There were times when friends and family failed them, or when young people felt they had let themselves down. Under these circumstances immanent faith was threatened, and it was often to a cultural memory of Christian belief and practice that our young people then turned to piece together a working spirituality that was private, subjectively orientated and often transient. This spirituality could provide the necessary immediate assurance and hope to 'go on'. The young people's relationship with the Church and Christianity resonated with Davie's description of vicarious religion: the beliefs, symbols, rituals and traditions held and sustained by a few were available to others when needed. The clearest expression of this spiritual engagement was young people's accounts of praying in their bedrooms alone, last thing at night. We call this 'bedroom spirituality'.

Immanent faith

Several years ago we had a conversation with Lisa, a teenager living in the south-east of England. When asked about her faith Lisa said, 'I love me and my family and friends. No other Gods. I believe in myself' (Collins 1997). This comment would not have been out of place among the young people in the present study.

Family and friends

The importance of family and close friends to our young people, whether they were churchgoers or not, was unmistakeable. When asked to identify the most important thing in life in an open question on the Phase 1 questionnaire, 53% wrote family and 57% friends. We gained a sense of the faith young people put in these relationships from their comments during the interviews. Jill, for example, said, 'you are nothing without your family'. For Zac, 'family are there when you need them'. They are 'what gets you through the day' (Harry). 'You're not really nothing without your family' (Linda). In short, 'you can't do no better than family' (Bernadette). As for friends, Addie said that she would be 'in a real mess without friends'. Rachel, a frequent churchgoer, reserved the word 'faith' for her trust in God, but placed friendship next on the list: 'I, as a person, value friendship because as well as my faith, my friends are always there when I'm down, things like that, it's really good.'

Our young people identified different ways in which family and friends helped them feel secure in the world. Since all of the young people were living with at least one family member or relative, families were a source of material support. Beyond that, however, the young people appreciated family and close friends because they provided moral support in times of difficulty or when they were worried about something and needed someone to talk to (see Table 3.1). Rachel illustrates the point. She was clear that if she were worried about something she would talk to her mum straightaway.

> She's brilliant, she's there when I wake up, there when I come home, yeah she's definitely the first person I would go to. She's brilliant with everything and she knows – like I said, she's been there, done that, so she knows exactly what I'm going through. Every situation I'm in she's been through it, which is really helpful cos she's got on-hand experience. It's brilliant, yeah.

Table 3.1 Which of the following people do you feel you could comfortably talk to if something was worrying you?

	Frequent churchgoers** % 'yes'	Infrequent churchgoers** % 'yes'
Parents	51	49
Other family members	22	23
Friends	72	74
Teachers	7	6
Religious leaders*	14	3
Youth workers*	46	20

* Statistically significant difference between the two groups (p<0.05)
** Percentages rounded to the nearest whole number.

Clive confirmed that 'family and friends help you through times when you just want to give up and stuff . . . Like depression and stuff.' For Ed, his aunt would be his confidante 'because she's really nice and she understands everything, and doesn't make fun of me if there's something a bit weird or crazy.' Vera would speak to her parents

> Cos they don't tell anyone; but my friends do . . . Like if I fancy a boy they will tell them that I fancy them . . . All my friends they'd tell all my secrets, but my family won't say anything.

The emotional support of family and friends helped to confer on the young person a positive sense of self as somebody who is known and both acceptable and accepted, someone who *belongs*. As Karen put it, family 'will always be there for you, even though you have your ups and downs'. 'They [family] know you through your daily experiences of life' (Rachel).

> Having a good family [is important], because I would hate to be alone, I wouldn't be able to handle it and I just think you always need someone there to talk to (Hilary).

Taken together, the young people's comments indicated criteria for trustworthiness similar to those identified in our earlier work (Collins 1997:126). In the young people's eyes the sort of person one could trust and have faith in:

- had the young person's best interests at heart;
- understood the young person's situation;
- was willing to help, if appropriate, either practically through informed advice or just being somebody who would listen to them whilst they worked through issues for themselves;

- would respect confidentiality;
- would not place guilt or shame on the young person.[1]

Of course, not all family members or friends were trusted equally, and some individuals within families were not trusted at all. In this respect, some of our young people had very difficult home lives.[2] Moreover, few individuals fully met all the above criteria of trustworthiness all of the time, so the young people were apt to weigh up which of these components were most important in any one situation. For example, sometimes friends were the trusted confidants when they were seen as having more understanding of the young person's situation than parents would have, friends being of a similar age and going through similar things to the young person herself. At other times family were preferred when they were seen as being in a position to provide better advice or as being less likely to laugh at and shame the young person than their friends would be.[3]

There was, however, some blurring between the designation of family and friends. The young people would sometimes talk of their best friends as being family, and of family members as being friends. Cecilia said of her best friend (who although male was not her boyfriend in the romantic sense): 'he's like a brother really. I can literally tell him everything, everything I can tell my mum or my cousin I can tell him.' She went on to describe her cousin and also her mum as her best friends. Gary described his uncle as 'one of my friends . . . he's like more than an uncle.' Addie's sister was 'pretty much like a friend'.

Duncan and Phillips (2008) argue that increasingly parents are looking for an extended involvement in their children's lives. This means that they befriend their children and end up taking the role of 'critical companion' which has traditionally been the role of the youth worker. Parents encourage their children in their life choices and accompany them through different stages of personal and social development. In adopting what we might call 'friendship parenting', parents and children become locked together in a type of intergenerational youth club where each reflects back the importance of the other. The young person is affirmed and the parent is validated. This view echoes Hervieu-Léger's observation that late modern families prioritize emotion over heritage, thereby making them vulnerable to instability when members are no longer emotionally satisfied. She distinguishes between late modern families and traditional families which have a deeper sense of historical continuity:

> The 'club' family gives prime consideration to the autonomy of its individual members; it is based on a realistic assessment of the assets and constraints

of life in common. The family as history is based on an interweaving of emotional solidarity and a pact of continuity consciously made by its members (2001:134).

From this we can note two things. First, this loss of continuity at the family level in late modern society potentially contributes to the broader loss of cultural memory elsewhere. People get out of the habit of remembering and traditions fade. Second, just as the Christian faith is undermined by breaks in the lineage of belief, so immanent faith can be threatened and disrupted by discontinuities in intimate relationships. This does not mean that faith disappears but, just as with religious faith, it becomes selectively renegotiated. Our young people were, and had to be, quite adept at developing their own networks of trust, drawing on selected members of the extended family when the immediate family was not up to the task. Step-parents, brothers, sisters, grandparents, aunts and uncles could all take up the role of the trusted other if biological parents let them down or were absent. To pick up on Hervieu-Léger's idea of 'elective fraternities' mentioned in Chapter 1, we could say that young people constructed an elective fraternity drawing upon existing extended family structures as well as peer relations. In this respect it was the parenting role rather than the parenting person who provided stability and security – the faith to live by. Duncan and Philips (2008) concur that caring and loving relationships are consciously developed and built up on the basis of what they do rather than depending on the given biological or kinship status. Steve provides just one of many examples from our young people:

> He [step-dad] always goes up to the school with me when I was getting bullied and he helped me out. And I didn't want to tell my mum or dad or family because I felt they would think that – what people had done to me, I thought they'd think that I'm a wimp and I can't stand up for myself and stuff like that. I thought they'd think I was a bit lower than them. So I told him [step-dad] and he sorted it all out and he didn't tell my mum and my dad until I wanted him to tell them.

The variety of family structures identified amongst our young people reflects something of the range and fluidity of family forms nationally. UNICEF (2007) ranked child wellbeing in Britain as the lowest of 21 industrialized countries because of its high rate of single-parent and step-families. However, the report also indicates that the percentage of children who reported eating the main meal of the day with parents and spending time 'just talking' to them was in the top half of the 21 countries. For many of our young people, it would seem that this latter measure would be of more immediate concern in terms of maintaining immanent faith.

Self

As well as trusting in family and friends, the young people also spoke of the need to believe and trust in themselves. The individualization of late modern society has been inculcated in their minds. Colin put it like this when asked what was most important in life: 'Faith in yourself, cos if you don't have faith in yourself, then you're not going to be able to do anything whereas you'd like to.'

Faith in self required self-knowledge, authenticity and a degree of self-realization. For Alicia, acquiring self-knowledge was achieved in a practical manner to find out what 'fits' – 'I don't think you know yourself and you need to find a way to get to know yourself ... do things that you like and things that you don't like.' In this way, Alicia could discover her true authentic self and realize her full potential. For many, the youth club provided opportunities for self-development.[4]

During the interviews we asked the young people if they thought life had an ultimate purpose. Here again self-reliance was evident. Many of them thought it was up to them to make up or find their own purpose. Jack told his youth worker he had an opportunity to fulfil his dreams but he 'has to push hard to achieve ... you've got to work really hard at it.' Callum put it more bluntly: 'Purpose is the thing that we work for and strive towards. I decide what my purpose is by weighing up the positives and negatives. Nobody else tells me what it is.' Emma's thoughts were similar: 'you make it happen, you choose your own destiny.' Many of the young people thought that the purpose of life was to live it 'to the max' and that meant being proactive – 'like doing all the stuff you can ... take every opportunity' (Ed).

The young people also demonstrated faith in their self through the importance they placed on autonomous decision-making. They did not like being told what to do. We develop our discussion around this theme in Chapter 5 when we consider the outworking of faith in daily life and ethical choices.

Make do and mend

Immanent faith sustained our young people's everyday lives and, for the infrequent churchgoers at least, was quite sufficient most of the time. They were not looking beyond the 'here and now'. God and religion were largely irrelevant to them. In our survey 81% of the infrequent churchgoers said that they thought about God only 'occasionally or never', and when they did think about God or religion it tended to be as a result of an external prompting such as a religious education class at school, a conversation with a youth worker, a television programme or a visit to a church for a family event (see Chapter 4). Usually religious thinking at these times was abstract and concerned with what other people think and do rather than the young person's own beliefs. And yet, despite general indifference most of the time, every so often the young people did wonder at what lies beyond this world and the personal relevance of religious beliefs to themselves. These occasions tended to be private moments. Sometimes they occurred when the young person had nothing else to do; otherwise it was late at night just before going to sleep. 'Sometimes when I'm sitting down bored and watching telly I think about how did we get here' (Tristan). '[I] normally [think about God] ... at night, when I go to bed on my own, when it's really quiet' (Wendy). 'I think it's really relaxing just going to sleep, alone with your thoughts and you can figure things out. I often think about why we're here' (Martin). In this respect religious faith was seen as a private concern and did not form a routine part of everyday conversation. Even frequent churchgoers, who often think through their beliefs and were more open about them, were nevertheless selective about when and with whom they discussed their Christian faith.

Under normal circumstances the infrequent churchgoers' private musings did not move much beyond mild curiosity – 'I wonder if' type thinking. However, occasionally religious considerations did become more urgent and that was when they, their family or friends faced a serious difficulty. At this point immanent faith was under threat and the cultural memory of Christianity became a spiritual resource from which to derive meaning and comfort in order to shore up or restore their sense of ontological security.

> In the last year religion's really come into my family because we've had a few bereavements, my cousin might have meningitis, my mum's pregnant, and it's like, well, what's going to happen? So they are praying to God, saying 'Please everything's gonna be alright.' (Barry)

It was a case of spiritual 'make do and mend' – the young people had to make do with the cultural memory of Christianity in the absence of other religious or spiritual resources, to mend immanent faith.

Christian beliefs

Our survey and discussions with young people gave us a flavour of the cultural memory they were drawing upon. The young people's image of God was often reminiscent of representations of Christian stories in popular culture. God was routinely described in masculine terms, as being powerful, somehow related to the Bible and sometimes as an old man with a beard. 'He's the main man' said Lola. 'Six foot, got a beard, wearing a gown' (Finlay). 'God is vengeful, giving, caring, and loving' (Bradley). 'He has long white hair. He's kind and soft . . . you know, nice and spiritual. I think God protects you' (Robert).

As is to be expected, the frequent churchgoers were more likely to hold an understanding of God that fitted with the traditional Christian teaching of a God who can be known personally (see Table 3.2). The constellation of emotionally satisfying intimate relations that was characteristic of immanent faith was reflected in how some of the frequent churchgoers talked about God, in that God was seen as more friend than authority figure. Amelia told her youth worker, 'I'm buzzing with God at the moment. He's a good friend of mine, we're mates, we're happy, I love him.' Anthony also described God as his friend, as did Morgan and Lily: 'he's like my best friend and my father and everything. Not like other people.' On the other hand, some of the young people, more especially the infrequent churchgoers, preferred to think of God as a 'higher power', 'spirit' or 'essence' which contrasted with personified images of God, but they still spoke of this as a beneficent Higher Power which was external to the self rather than a God 'within'. In this respect overall half (53%) of the infrequent churchgoers in our

Table 3.2 Perceptions of God and Jesus

	Frequent church-goers* % agree	Infrequent church-goers* % agree	All young people in the survey* % agree
Which one of the following statements comes closest to your belief about God?**			
I believe in a God who is someone I can know personally.	76	23	53
I believe in some sort of Higher Power or Life Force, but not in a personal God.	10	22	15
I don't really know what to think.	13	43	27
I don't think there is any sort of God, Higher Power or Life Force.	1	12	6
Who do you think Jesus Christ is/was?**			
A very wise person	5	21	12
An ordinary person	1	9	5
The Son of God	87	31	62
Someone who never existed	0	8	3
I don't know	5	27	15
Other	2	4	3

* Figures rounded to the nearest whole number.
** Statistically significant difference between the two groups (p<0.05)

survey[5] agreed that 'it is comforting at times to believe in God'; only 21% disagreed.

When we asked the infrequent churchgoers which Bible stories they knew, they could name some of the most famous ones and a few biblical figures – 'feeding of the five thousand', 'water into wine', 'burning bush', 'Noah and the world being destroyed', 'Moses', 'the Last Supper' – but they did not always know the details of the story. Sienna summed up the extent of her familiarity with biblical stories: '[I know] the main one, how he [Jesus] was born and how he died and rose again. The Easter and the Christmas stories, these are the only main stories that I really know'.

The lack of detailed biblical knowledge echoes the findings of the National Biblical Literacy Survey (Beavan 2009), but the fact that there was a vague awareness of stories at all does point to the existence, albeit very faint, of a cultural Christian memory for young people to access. This was further confirmed during a couple of the youth work sessions when some of the infrequent churchgoing youth were asked to comment on a range of different pictures of Jesus designed in part to challenge the viewer. The young people generally preferred images which fitted with their positive and 'nice' image of Jesus which they were aware of from wider cultural representations. A picture of an angry Jesus was met with 'Jesus was never like that' by Finlay. According to Cameron, Jesus 'walks with authority, presence and [is] really nice as well'. He did not like a picture of Jesus hugging a woman as that made Jesus 'a player', that is to say, one for the ladies. Lola liked a South Park cartoon of Jesus which tapped into cultural stereotypes of straggly hair, a little goatee beard and a yellow halo. Mervyn on the other hand thought that the cartoon was 'taking the mick out of someone's religion and belief' which he really did not like.

The young people were therefore aware of a cultural Christian memory, but they were quite vague about its details and most, especially those who were infrequent churchgoers, had a very low level of engagement with it. In fact, as Table 3.2 shows, around two in five of our infrequent churchgoers said they did not know what they believed about God, and around one in four did not know what they thought about Jesus. Yet in times of crisis many of our young people seemed to 'make do' with this faint memory on a 'need to believe' basis. For some it was the only point of religious reference they had, for others it was supplemented with one or two religious-cum-spiritual ideas found in popular culture. That said, there were only a few references to alternative spiritualities or the beliefs of other world faiths during the course of our interviews.

Alternative beliefs

Andrew said he had some spell books and had been 'practising spells from those'. Cecilia had practised 'pink magic' before and had a passing interest in the Nation of Islam having read a book by Malcolm X, but is now Christian. In any case, she said, pink magic has 'got quite a lot to do with Jesus ... 'cos it mentions like God and Jesus'. Amanda wrote to her guardian angel by way of her diary every night. Only Hilary had a really eclectic mix of beliefs which she seemed to have inherited from her mother. She would have 'loved to have been an ancient Egyptian', she said, and believed in aliens, fairies and leprechauns because 'it's cool to believe in other stuff. Just because you haven't seen one doesn't mean it's not there.' But these beliefs, she conceded, do not affect her daily life although they did make her feel a little more 'unique' compared to other people. Beyond that, the 'pick and mix' spirituality which is often referred to by commentators on contemporary religion was largely restricted to ideas about reincarnation, karma and ghosts, and these beliefs could be as tentative as those associated with Christianity. Yet, like Christian ideas, these alternatives became significant when the young people were faced with the most unsettling and difficult times of all – namely those associated with death, dying and bereavement.

Death

Death and what happens after we die was a recurrent theme brought up by the young people throughout the interviews but particularly in relation to their interest in 'spirituality' – a word which was not immediately understood by many of our young people, but which, when encouraged to think about it, they associated with ghosts, God and the afterlife. The young people in this respect indicated a moderate interest in spirituality. Julie, for example, told her youth worker, 'I am intrigued about dying ... and what may be there afterwards'. Jill sometimes asked herself, 'am I going to be with God when I die?' Bradley had been concerned about 'dying and the world coming to an end' when he was younger. Alice said, 'Death is direct. There's no getting around it, it's the only thing you can be sure of.'

Death in late modern society can be hard to understand. Life expectancy in Britain has increased progressively over the last 25 years (ONS 2009b) which means that it is mainly the very old who die. Moreover, in the normal course of events death is sequestered away in hospitals and hospices, and handled by professionals so that the dying process itself is outside of most young people's experiences. The proliferation of violent and glamourized representations of death in video games, television programmes and films tends to anaesthetize young people to its reality. Even responsible reporting of death in the news media can have the effect of flattening its significance since stories quickly switch from one item to the next. Notwithstanding all this, young people are periodically brought up short by the death of somebody they know personally or through the media. For example the death of Steve Erwin, the Australian naturalist and entertainer, had affected a couple of our young people because it made them aware that 'you can just go anytime' (Letitia). Several of the young people mentioned losing a grandparent, a parent, a sibling or a friend – the latter included violent deaths. Indeed, one of the interviews had to be stopped part way through as a shooting incident took place outside the youth club. When death is close at hand questions about the nature of God and the afterlife are brought into sharper focus:

> Sometime I wonder if God's really there and I look at the sky at night time, I look up and see if I can see anything, and I'm like, 'Yeah, God is really there'; and sometimes I'm like, 'If God's really there, why's he making people die of things?'; like my brother got stabbed. (Nials)

Of course, one of the functions of the Church has traditionally been to make sense of and manage death within a community. In the Christian tradition, the chain of believers includes the saints who have gone before and we look forward to meeting them again at the second coming. Burials and graveyards provided a tangible reminder of this in a way that cremations and scattered ashes do not.

As we note in Chapter 1, the majority of deaths in Britain are still marked by a Christian funeral. However, because much of the Christian memory has faded so have the traditional discourse, symbols and rituals of death, leaving questions unanswered for our young people. The cultural unease with death and dying was brought home in the public spectacle of Jade Goody's battle with terminal cancer (2009). The public interest was a result of Goody's celebrity status but can also be seen as an example of society trying to work out its relationship to death in the absence of a common understanding. The public debate around assisted suicide is another example.

As new ways of making sense of death are established, so too are new rituals for marking and managing it. The public mournings that followed the Hillsborough Disaster in 1989 and the death of Princess Diana in 1997 are well documented (e.g. Davie 1993 and Walter 1999) and shows how Christian belief and tradition became blended with secular markers of community and identity. It is now common to see flowers, candles and soft toys laid at the site of death or places of personal significance to the deceased, as well as at the site of burial (Barley 2006:27). Young people have picked up on this. During the course of writing up our research, for instance, we witnessed memorial graffiti on a wall at the site of a young person's murder. Bob also took a memorial service for a young person where the choice of music selected by the bereaved was entirely pop songs because the young congregation did not know any hymns. And yet, even in this instance of a highly personalized service the Church, its traditions and, indeed, the church building still had residual authority. Blended with the personal, this authority mattered to the congregation since it carried with it a sense of solemnity and propriety which translates into respect and honour for the deceased – it was about taking death seriously. Davie's (2007a) point that the Church remains important for providing rituals is well grounded even for young people when it came to death. Totally subjective rituals are not enough on their own; a communal response to death backed by the authority of tradition is required as well.

Outside of the Church, our young people's attempts to make sense of death were disjointed and confused. They drew in part on ideas of God and an afterlife vaguely related to the Christian memory – Colin said, 'Without God everyone's scared of dying'. Lola mentioned the idea of purgatory with God deciding if you go to heaven or hell. Kian said he was interested in Christianity because 'I don't want to go to hell'. Ashley made the same point:

> I really do believe in hell, hell and a heaven . . . people say that you can't have committed any sins in your life [if you are to go to heaven] but that's not true because if that was the reason I wouldn't be there so . . . But I believe that as you're going up to heaven then God will ask you why you have committed those sins and for each sin you've done . . . he will punish Jesus, as Jesus sacrificed himself for all the sins, that's what I believe.

Hilary on the other hand did not believe in heaven and hell, just as she rejected belief in the virgin birth and creation stories, while Wendy thought, 'you go to heaven, everybody . . . apart from evil people . . . I think everybody would have a different heaven, it would be like where you positioned yourself'. Some, particularly if they were infrequent churchgoers like Barry, preferred the idea of reincarnation (see Table 3.3).

> See I believe that there is another world, but I believe there is like a reincarnation bit of it. If you're good you're going to come back as something good, if you're bad you're going to come back as something horrible.

Reincarnation tended to be a standalone reference, however – it was not linked by the young people into a wider religious tradition.

Table 3.3 What do you think happens to people when they die?*

	Frequent church-goers** % agree	Infrequent church-goers** % agree	All young people in the survey** % agree
Everyone goes to heaven	7	11	9
Good people go to heaven and bad people go to hell	25	13	20
Only Christians go to heaven	41	6	25
People die and are born again as someone or something else	6	25	15
Nothing, everything just stops	1	16	7
I'm not sure	19	30	24
Other	1	0	0

* Statistically significant difference between the two groups (p<0.05)
** Figures rounded to the nearest whole number.

The other main way of thinking about death was in terms of ghosts. Several of the young people said they had seen or experienced a ghost, often associated with dead grandparents. Andrew, following the use of a ouija board, thought he saw 'a face and some mist' which he took to be his dead grandmother – even though he had never met her, he 'just knew it was his grandma'. Alice interpreted the ghost of her grandmother watching over and guiding her as a 'guardian angel'. She described an incident to her youth worker. Alice had gone to a night club . . .

> . . . and she felt that it was really important at one point to get her and all her four other friends who were there with her into the toilet at one particular point. And she did. She made sure that she got everyone in the toilet and then as she did that there was a kind of stampede to get out of the place because someone had been shot or something. And she said, you know, she felt that there was something outside her telling her to do that, and she felt that's her dead nanna that guides her (Carlie, youth worker).

The important point about ghosts is that they provide continuity between the living and the dead, and in the absence of a Christian chain of memory, ghosts can provide a local family-centric chain that keeps the memory of the person alive and as such sustains immanent faith. Another common means of sustaining faith was through prayer.

Prayer life[6]

Despite the lack of engagement with the Christian tradition there was one area where young people did retain the traces of Christian memory and that was in terms of prayer. Sixty per cent of our young people said that they prayed at least monthly, and 22% at least occasionally. The proportion of pray-ers, as might be expected, was higher among frequent churchgoers, but a quarter even of the infrequent churchgoers said they prayed at least once a month and a further third that they prayed less than once a month but occasionally. This left just over a third of infrequent churchgoers who never said a prayer. The prevalence of prayer is not unique to our young people.[7] Francis and Robbins (2006) record that 29% of non-churchgoing 13 to 15 year olds pray at least occasionally and 3% almost daily.

For our young people prayers were occasioned in both public and private settings and this provided a notionally Christian template for the form prayers might take. Schools and youth clubs provided opportunities for prayer (Chapter 4) – schools through assemblies and sometimes in class, youth clubs through prayerful spaces and as part of routine activities. Given the absence of young people in the institutional Church, it was interesting to hear some young people say that they did join in these moments of 'public' prayer quite freely.

> Jack: And in the morning when we go to school . . . one person's got to pray every day . . . And everyone does it.
>
> Interviewer: Yeah? And how do you feel about doing that?
>
> Jack: I feel like it's good to do.
>
> . . . before club starts, cos they're all religious they pray. You don't have to join in but I just . . . pray as well (Colin).

Bedroom spirituality

On the whole, however, the young people's prayer activities were private, something which was done alone, at night in the bedroom. The location is significant. The bedroom is often the first space in which young people are able to exert some control, be creative and make their own. Lincoln (2005) describes how young women actively organize their bedrooms to create and recreate identity, meaning and motivation. She says that throughout their teenage years, the bedroom is a site of multiple cultural and social articulations and expressions. It is a space in which their cultural biography can be nurtured.

The foundations for bedroom prayers were sometimes set down in early child-hood by parents and grandparents. For example, Lance explained that, 'When my granddad phones me up every night yeah, he says are you praying on your bed?' Cathy as a frequent churchgoer tried to set aside time each evening for prayer, 'I usually pray in the evenings, I don't know why I pray in the evenings, cos I find it hard to get up in the mornings. It's basically a quiet time for me and God'. Many of the infrequent churchgoers echoed this practice, though their prayers were more sporadic. Letitia, for example, told her youth worker she'd prayed 'at night in her bedroom, on her own', as did Dylan, Emma and Zara. Rachel confessed, 'I do say a little prayer every night'. Zoe prays 'when I'm in bed or I turn the light out and I look at the stars'. Amanda said, 'It's usually when I'm alone probably just before I go to sleep. I don't know, it's quite personal for me – anything that's happened in the day, anything serious, I'll mull it over in my mind and just pray about it.'

The types of prayers the young people prayed in private were sometimes explicitly linked to institutional Christianity. For example, some mentioned saying the Lord's Prayer or Hail Mary. The majority, however, prayed more spontaneously but largely conformed to the Christian pattern of prayer they had experienced elsewhere. The young people's prayers loosely fell into three categories – (a) petitionary prayers, (b) confessional prayers and (c) prayers of thanksgiving.

Petitionary prayers

Petitionary prayers were concerned with eliciting help in difficult situations. The remit of these prayers reflected the local nature of immanent faith in that they tended to focus heavily on family, friends and the self. Thus prayers were said when family or friends were ill, in danger or dying; or when things went wrong for the young person him- or herself, arguments with friends, facing exams or feeling 'down in the dumps'. These prayers were often urgent, 'front-line' prayers, and in some cases prayers of last resort. As Russell enthusiastically put it, 'I pray when I want a miracle, when I want to complete a mission of James Bond!' Emma on the other hand prays in times of trouble; when she 'couldn't do anything else' she 'prays just in case'. Very few of our young people mentioned praying for people more widely or for world situations in their private prayers.

Through petitionary prayers young people could gain a sense of control and order over otherwise potentially chaotic and frightening situations. A sister with meningitis makes it clear that life is fragile, ultimately beyond individual control and that there is the potential for one being alone in the world. In other words, a family member with serious problems highlights the limitations of immanent faith. Petitionary prayers for our young people brought to mind a different reality which suggests that while life on earth is fragile there is more beyond it, that ultimately the world is ordered and that one is not alone.

Immanent faith was therefore extended, even if only temporarily, to include transcendent, notionally Christian, faith referents.

Prayer for our young people involved the work of holding in mind oneself, another person or situation and bringing them into symbolic relationship with God. Prayer is 'a way of talking to God, one to one' (Toby), 'a way to ask God for something' (James). 'I just have a talk with the Big Man upstairs' (Barry). Conversely, 'I don't believe in God so therefore there's no need for prayer' (Skye). In other words prayer was a legitimate, distinctive and deliberate action that young people chose to do or not. It was generally distinguishable from simply 'hoping for the best', 'wishful thinking' or 'self-talk', though these might run closely alongside praying.

> I think eighty per cent of what I do when I pray is thinking and talking. It's not actually religious. Praying, I guess, is twenty per cent of the time. I do actually ask God about it. (Amelia)

> I don't necessarily pray. But I sometimes hope that things will happen, but I don't see it as praying. (Polly)

> I'm not likely to pray at all, but at times I would. I wouldn't say I pray, I guess I talk to the air really. Because I've been brought up with God and that, so I still kind of have the odd chat now and again, but only every so often, like every blue moon. (Bradley)

As a deliberate action petitionary prayers were worth engaging in because they 'worked' at least insofar as the young person felt better for having prayed and 'done' something about a problem that was in their power to do. As such, prayers had a calming and relaxing effect on the young person. It was interesting to note that praying was not always dependent on believing that God existed. Day's (2010) analysis of young people's construction of belief draws attention to the work of Ruel (1982) and others in distinguishing propositional belief – 'belief-that' God exists – and faith orientated belief – 'belief-in' God. The latter is an action rather than a cognitive construct and it is the latter which restores ontological security. From the perspective of vicarious religion (see Chapter 1) we can say that it was enough that the young people knew others believed that a loving God exists for belief-in God to be kept open as a possibility for them. Vicarious 'belief-that' made prayer among even some of our least religious young people a plausible and authentic action.

The practice of prayer was quite resilient. If, however, the young people did not feel better after praying or did not see the general circumstances surrounding their prayer change, this could put them off future prayer; it eroded the potential of vicarious belief and undermined Christian faith.

Confessional prayers

The second type of prayers fell into the category of 'confession', or more generally 'reflection'. Confession as a spiritual practice has traditionally involved the self acknowledging and repenting of moral failing before God (sometimes mediated through a priest) and in that act finding forgiveness, healing of the soul and reconciliation with God and the wider community of the Church.

In late modern society the need to establish an authentic and acceptable self is a pressing one and an important aspect of immanent faith, but the idea of forgiveness and by whom, for what and within which community is less clear. The Church as an institution no longer has the authority to define what is true and acceptable, nor does it have exclusive control over the means by which this might ultimately be achieved. Instead individuals are increasingly left to work this out for themselves as part of the reflexive project of the self. The result has been a proliferation of 'confessional' activities which allow individuals to speak out the 'truth' about themselves to an 'other' (real or virtual) in an attempt to lay aside anxiety and negative emotions and find a valid, acceptable and accepted self. Indeed, commentators such as Foucault (1990) have argued that we have become an altogether 'confessing society'. It is easy to think of examples. Counsellors and psychotherapists take on the role of priest, listening to troubled souls and helping their clients engage in the emotional work towards wholeness. Reality television and chat shows feed on the participants' displays of emotional highs and lows but promise 'salvation' through fame and the social acceptance awarded by a judging audience. Social networking sites, blogs and tweets, provide further opportunities for 'self narration' to whoever logs on; the number of 'friends' and 'hits' on these sites provide an instant account of the interest others are taking and one's level of social acceptance and belonging in a community. Yet for all this, our young people indicated it was their private prayerful 'confessions' and reflections in the safety of their own bedroom that provided a means by which they could work towards a valid and coping self.

The traditional language associated with religious confessions was only used by a minority of our young people:

> Sometimes when I pray I think I may not have said sorry for the last sin I did ... it may not have been counted. God knows I'm probably sorry anyway. (Maisie)

> I pray all the time because, like, God created us and everything, and if you sin you go to hell. I don't want to go to hell. (Lily)

> Blake told his youth worker 'If he'd done something wrong then he'd kind of just chuck a quick prayer up there'.

The language of personal reflection – making truthful admissions about the self, dealing with self-anxieties, and reorientating a failing or struggling self – were more evident in the young people's descriptions of prayers. Our young people spoke of praying as a means of 'getting things off their chest', 'getting things out of their system', they felt 'listened to', and a 'weight being lifted', 'calm' and 'relaxed'. God was the intended recipient for these confessions of self. In this respect God tended to be seen as a confidant rather than judge, a figure wholly meeting the criteria of trustworthiness listed above. To borrow an apt phrase from psychotherapy, God's presence in these circumstances was experienced as one of 'hovering attentiveness' (Cox 1990).

> If you're struggling – everybody struggles in life – sometimes you just need someone. Even though you've got your family and friends to talk to, it sometimes just feels [like] you need somebody else to talk to, so you talk to God. (Karen)

> Regardless of whether He exists or not, if you're going through a problem and you're explaining them to whoever you believe in, it's got to be good. (Elvis)

> Prayer for me is getting things off my chest. It's talking to God. When you do you feel that you are listened to and not judged. (Callum)

God's role was to support and nurture a struggling or shamed self; absolving the guilt of moral failings was secondary. Through acts of self-confession, however, the young people could become more cognizant of their 'ideal self', and take some responsibility for movement in that direction. Ashley, for example, said that he prays when he has not 'pulled up to my full potential'. Frank suggested God sometimes 'reveals something to you about yourself, what you should be doing, changing and stuff'. Rachel said sorry to God for having said 'some bad things' to her friends and prayed for 'the strength to make up with them'.

Prayers of thanksgiving

The Christian pattern of prayer that young people learn as they grow up normally includes thanksgiving. Thanksgiving is a somewhat countercultural act in our society. Consumerism relies on dissatisfaction and the need to be constantly moving on to the next, better thing. The increasing social emphasis on individual rights and self-reliance diminishes a sense of social connectedness and grace – what is mine *should* be mine, what I've achieved I've achieved myself. This leaves little room for giving thanks to other people let alone God. Gratitude certainly is not an attitude that is normally associated with young people as they are portrayed in the media, yet a small minority of our young people did include thanksgiving in their prayers, even if it was only a prelude to getting on with the real business of asking for help:

> Oh yeah, I pray. It's not always negative, like if I'm praying everyday, obviously there's not dramas in my life every day, so when I pray ... like today I'm happy, so it's going to be about thanking God for today, thanking him for my friends, my cousin. (Cecilia)
>
> I pray to thank God and asking him for stuff as well. (Iain)
>
> If a bad thing happens I really concentrate on something, but if it's thanking, if it's been a good day, then it's just thanking and I don't really concentrate as much as I would if something really bad had happened. (Rachel)

Indeed, the template of prayer itself can prompt young prayers to stop and think, if just for a moment, about the benefits of life that they enjoy. Linda, for example, said saying thanks in her prayers 'makes me feel like I've appreciated my life, what's going on'. Simon surprised his youth worker by noting that the prayer time at the beginning of youth club football matches was 'a chance to be grateful'. The young people's comments suggested that a sense of gratitude in prayers can be beneficial to them as individuals – it helped them to appreciate life and gain a sense of perspective. More than this, however, a sense of gratitude is important for societal functioning as well. Simmel (1950:389) described gratitude as the 'moral memory of mankind' (1950:388) which binds people together and Emmons (2001) argues that gratitude is a vital civic virtue which motivates and sustains pro-social behaviour. Dylan illustrates the point. He told his youth worker that when he lies in bed at night and realizes how fortunate he is compared to other people, he then prays for others and their needs. 'Praying is good,' he said, 'it gets you thinking about those I'm better off than. Gets me thinking about giving to charity and poverty and all that stuff.'

Everyday faith

From the above we can see that young people's faith for living is derived from different sources. For all the young people family, friends and authentic, reflexive self were key components of a constellation of faith which we have called 'immanent faith'. Beyond this, for those who regularly participated in a believing Christian community, faith extended to the transcendent but it still mirrored some of the properties of faith at the immanent level in that the emphasis tended to be on a subjectively rewarding relationship with God. For the rest, the infrequent churchgoers, some managed without any reference to religion – immanent faith was enough. For the majority, some recourse to religion was periodically necessary and under these circumstances more often than not the Christian memory was their point of reference. A memory kept alive by a minority, a memory that was very faded and largely unexamined, but nonetheless an important dimension to faith when it was needed most. In the next chapter we consider the processes of faith transmission by which young people learn about Christianity and gain what is left of the cultural memory.

4

Lost in transmission

Faith does not emerge on its own, it always develops in a social context. The Christian memory is most effectively kept alive by believing faith communities living out their story and actively passing it on to each new generation through their embodied traditions and education processes (Ammerman 2006:46, Martin 2002). However, most young people, like the infrequent churchgoers in our study, are not embedded in such communities and therefore inherit only a faint Christian memory from wider culture. Much of the doctrinal and credal substance as understood by the Church is missing, but it is this memory which often is the main point of religious or spiritual reference young people turn to in times of trouble. Perhaps somewhat disappointingly from a Church point of view, this faint Christian memory seemed good enough for our young people to get by on. There was little evidence of their searching out other faiths to take up the religious or spiritual slack left in the absence of a more substantive engagement with Christianity. In this chapter we explore how it is that infrequent churchgoing young people come to have their sense of Christianity and why they make do with a watered down version of the faith rather than search for religious or spiritual meaning and solace elsewhere.

Lack of hostility

We can note at the outset that very few of our young people were hostile to Christianity. Among those who rarely went to church we found the 'benign indifference' of the English towards religion (Fox 2004) rather than outright rejection. In fact, when Christianity was raised as a topic of conversation with our infrequent churchgoers they indicated mild interest. The basis of their interest revolved around three themes: (a) their own Christian identity even if somewhat nominal, (b) religion as part of life and society, and (c) Christianity as guidelines for living. These themes are interrelated but we will take each in turn and consider how, in the eyes of our young people, different social influences came to bear upon them, including of course the Christian youth work that we set out to study.

Identity

Identity refers to an individual's composite sense of self. It is informed by personal experiences and reflection, and socially ascribed characteristics and roles with their associated meanings. As we saw in Chapter 1, selfhood has become increasingly flexible and contingent. People can, to a much greater extent than in the past, construct their own identity and work on their 'project of self' (Giddens 1991). Identity is also a situated entity. In different contexts its various aspects become more or less salient. Our infrequent churchgoers did not have a strong sense of personal religious or spiritual identity most of the time. In the Phase 1 survey we included a question that asked which, if any, of a number of listed characteristics they would apply to themselves. Among these we included 'a spiritual person' and 'a religious person'. Only 9% of our infrequent churchgoers described themselves as 'spiritual', 5% as 'religious' and 5% as 'religious and spiritual'[1]. In fact we found that many of the young people did not have a clear idea of what 'spiritual' and 'spirituality' meant to them – these words were simply not part of their normal vocabulary (cf Rankin 2005:43). This left 81% of our infrequent churchgoers as neither spiritual nor religious. Nevertheless, just under half of the infrequent churchgoers in the survey affiliated themselves with Christianity – 29% Church of England, 5% Roman Catholic and 11% 'other' Christian.[2] This religious affiliation was an aspect of their social identity much as gender, ethnicity, age and class were. It contributed both to their sense of 'who I am' and to their sense of 'who I am not', and provided the main reference point when religious – and indeed spiritual – matters were raised. As such, religious affiliation carried some meaning for our infrequent churchgoers even though they rarely engaged with it in terms of formal religious participation. It also gave rise to a passing interest in Christianity.

Supporting the home team

The young people's Christian affiliation was primarily derived from two sources. For some there was recognition of a Christian heritage in England which they took to imply a Christian cultural identity of which they were a part. For example, James, who told us, 'even though I don't follow it, I am Christian,' was of the view that different religions are cultural variants of the same thing and his affiliation to Christianity reflected cultural loyalty. He used a football analogy – 'it's like everyone plays football but you support different teams and you don't want to support someone else's team because you don't live there'.

A stronger influence on the adoption of a Christian identity, however, was family background and upbringing. Our young people did not stray far beyond their initial religious socialization when it came to religious affiliation. Evie, for example, felt that Christianity was 'her religion' even though she did not go to church, because she 'had been brought up in it' by her grandparents – 'I've had an upbringing that incorporated God'. She therefore wanted to know more about it. Callum said, 'I am interested in Christianity since when I was young I went to church for a few years'.

Others, of course, had been brought up in a home indifferent to religion. So, while some young people thought of their family as Christian they were not entirely sure and rarely could they name their family's denominational associations. Ashley, for example, took a guess at his father's faith; 'It's mainly just Christian. I don't really know, because I don't really know his religion. I don't know if my family is one religion or they ain't religious.' Religion simply was not that important in his family. In fact, 21% of our infrequent churchgoers in the survey said they did not know their family's religion. Very few of our young people had an overtly anti-religious upbringing though. Alicia was one such exceptional case. She used to go to church with her mum, but when she stayed at her father's house he stopped her going to church 'because he didn't believe in it.' He also took her Bible away while her brother taunted her by saying, 'Oh God is brickdust!' She now described herself as 'lost' though she did still go to church very occasionally. In the main, however, if there was any anti-religious sentiment on the part of parents it simply manifested itself by the avoidance of having anything to do with religion. Grandparents then sometimes came in to fill the gap of religious transmission.

For some of our young people the fact of having been baptized in infancy conferred an identity which they were happy to own, even if they made little day-to-day reference to it. Sienna thought that being christened should make Jesus more relevant to her than he actually was. Thomas was not 'persuaded about Christianity' but referred to his christening to classify himself as '80% Christian'. The material effects associated with an individual's christening ceremony were sometimes infused with meaning linking Christian identity to personal biographies, family narratives and location. Karen, for instance, was keen to point out that the church she sometimes attends now is different to where she had been christened. 'I go to St James' ... But that's not the one I was christened at. I was Christened at a church at the Elephant and Castle

[London].' Andrew, who had been given a necklace with a picture of Jesus on it at his christening, chose to pass it on to his aunt to protect her on a trip to India. Caroline still had the dress she had been christened in. It may be that it had been passed down through the family from previous generations. In all these cases the Christian identity was passed on as part of the familial chain of memory, but the connection with church tradition weakened as each generation had less and less contact with a believing community.

The interesting point about religious affiliation derived from family ascriptions is that it goes against the tide of modern individualism. Constructing selfhood entails reflexive work on the part of the individual, opportunity and access to resources, and a degree of emotional, cognitive and social dexterity. For our infrequent churchgoers the apparently unreflexive acceptance of 'being Christian', together with their lack of religious engagement, suggests that many of our young people preferred to take the religious aspect of their identity for granted, either because to explore it further was not seen as a priority or because they lacked the resources or skills to do so. This was not a problem from the young people's point of view as this socially ascribed Christian identity sufficed for most purposes where religion was called for. It even left some of them positively disposed to learn more about it. Francis (1990) made a similar observation from his survey of 4948 eleven year olds. He found non-churchgoers who retained a Christian identity held a more positive attitude towards Christianity than those who did not.

The ascribed religious identity gave our young people a notional sense of connection with Christianity and church. In most cases, however, it would be stretching a point too far to say that this equated to a sense of Christian 'belonging' as such. Belonging requires emotional engagement, relationship and participation in a group or community. For the purposes of faith transmission, belonging is important because it is through embracing a community's language, customs, symbols and stories that identity is played out and reinforced. As far as Christianity is concerned this means that faith can only be passed on fully through participating in a church community where the full tradition is made available, however that is denominationally conceived at any particular time (traditions, after all, are not static entities either). Church in this sense provides a community of formation and Christian parents have a vital role to play in encouraging such participation by their children. Voas and Crockett sound a sobering note on this point in their analysis of religious change based on national survey data:

> If neither parent attends [church] at least once a month, the chances of the child doing so are negligible: less than 3 per cent. If both parents attend at

least monthly, there is a 46 per cent chance that the child will do so. Where just one parent attends, the likelihood is halved to 23 per cent. What these results suggest is that in Britain institutional religion now has a half-life of one generation, to borrow the terminology of radioactive decay. (2005:21)

Our infrequent churchgoers for the most part stood outside of a church community. They did, however, belong to two other communities of learning (if not quite 'formation') which they noted were (or had been) significant in resourcing and sustaining their Christian identity – namely their school and their youth club.

Embodied Christian identity

The English education system has strong historical links with the Church. Currently around a third of state schools in England are church schools, predominantly Church of England or Roman Catholic (Teachernet 2009), catering for about a quarter of pupils in the state system (Davie 2000:85). These are often popular with parents (religiously committed or not) partly because they tend to produce good academic results and partly because they are understood as providing a good moral ethos. Some church schools have a stronger Christian ethos than others. Both Davie (2000) and Kay and Francis (1996) note that historically the link between denomination and school has been stronger for the Roman Catholic Church than for the Church of England. Roman Catholic schools have traditionally aimed to provide a Catholic education for Catholic children to build up the Catholic faith community, whereas Church of England schools have been less denominationally focused and more concerned with a 'general theology of service to the nation' (Kay and Francis 1996:48). That said, Francis notes that the intake to Roman Catholic schools is now also quite mixed in terms of pupil belief and identity. Francis' own research and review of other studies indicates that while church schools can have a positive influence on young people's attitudes towards Christianity over and above any influence from home or church, this is not guaranteed (Kay and Francis 1996:44–58).

As far as our young people were concerned the significance of schools in informing Christian identity was apparent in that they provided an opportunity to learn about the Christian tradition through religious education (RE) classes, and with opportunities to participate in different aspects of the tradition through assemblies, classroom prayers, school Eucharists etc. This was true both for church schools and non-denominational state schools albeit to different degrees, because there is a statutory requirement for all state schools in England to make provision for acts of collective worship which are broadly of a

Christian nature.[3] Participation in religious activity is particularly important when it comes to identity if we accept that identity is not just conceptualized but also embodied. Through participating in Christian practices young people get a 'feel for' *being* Christian.[4] Indeed, practice can precede and outlast conceptual belief. We saw in the last chapter that prayer, for instance, was not dependent on belief that God exists, but in the doing of prayer God became a possibility. On the other hand, a young person can express *rejection* of a religious identity by withholding participation in worship activities. Either way identity is acted out.

Our young people gave various examples of schools providing opportunities for them to participate in Christian practices. Sienna said she had learnt to pray at infant school through assemblies and now knew the Lord's Prayer. She also remembered going to church for harvest festival. William told us, 'In assembly yeah, well they pray for us. Most people don't, but when they say, like, put your head down, think about it, I do think about it.' Addie went to a school where they had 'hymns every day and a chapel service once every month' and although she found that 'quite annoying', looking at the Bible did make her think. Jacqui went to a Roman Catholic secondary school. She prayed when she had to and went to Mass, but she did not take the wafer or the wine as, in her words, she is 'not really a Catholic'.

Take it or leave it

School religious practices lay down traces of the Christian memory to which young people can return if they want to and provide a point of reference for religious identity. Without school religion the Christian memory would be very much weaker than it currently is. However, the compulsory nature of religion in schools was sometimes experienced as imposed religion and this could undermine a young person's interest in Christianity. As Trili put it, 'It shouldn't be forced on us, we should learn it [Christianity] for ourselves. I'm not interested because I need to find my space to find it myself'. In this respect the youth clubs had an advantage over schools. While the majority of the young people knew the youth club had a Christian ethos and to different degrees clubs made provision for young people to engage in religious practices – prayers before youth work sessions, Christian camps away from the club, prayer rooms and quiet spaces in the club for personal prayer and reflection – the young people's participation was always experienced as voluntary. Tamsin described the situation in her club: 'They don't like to force any religion on you or try and talk to you about it if you don't go to them 'cause they know a lot of people don't want to talk about it.'

The downside of the voluntary nature of religious participation in terms of passing on and reinforcing the Christian memory is that many of the young people simply chose not to join in. They did not feel the need to since they already participated at school and religion was not that important to them. In any case, most of the young people were at the youth club to be with friends and socialize rather than to 'do' religion. None of the infrequent churchgoers who filled out the questionnaire in Phase 1 listed anything to do with religion as one of the things they liked best about the club. On the other hand, none of them said religion was the thing they liked least about the club either. They did, however, value the youth club as somewhere they could belong and build up a positive sense of identity in terms of general self-esteem. Several of the young people, for example, commented on how the youth club had helped them grow in confidence and enabled them to be themselves. Addie said the people at her youth club 'don't judge you. They just sort of accept you, who you are, and that's fine'. Hilary concurred. The youth club is somewhere you can 'be yourself and not get judged'. The Christian ethos was therefore just a background feature of the club for many of the infrequent churchgoing young people.

Nurturing frequent churchgoers' identity

Among the frequent churchgoers, however, the situation was rather different. For them the youth club, over and above school and church, was vital for supporting a positive sense of Christian identity. 15% of frequent churchgoers identified religious qualities as being part of what they liked most about their club. These included 'Bible study', 'making Christianity interesting', 'learning about God and Christianity', 'worshipping God'. Frequent churchgoers were more likely than infrequent churchgoers to say the club helped them learn about God, Jesus and the purpose of life (see Table 4.1), and to identify youth workers as helping them to think through their religious beliefs (Table 4.2). 70% of frequent churchgoers, compared to a quarter of infrequent churchgoers, said they would like more opportunities to learn about God.

Table 4.1 Has being a part of the youth group here caused you to think about any of the following?

	Frequent churchgoers* % Yes	Infrequent churchgoers* % Yes
What the purpose of life is**	54	28
God**	82	30
Jesus**	72	26
What is right and wrong	64	54

* Figures rounded to the nearest whole number.
** The difference between the two groups is statistically significant ($p<0.05$).

Table 4.2 Who helps you to think through your religious beliefs?

	Frequent churchgoers* % Yes	Infrequent churchgoers* % Yes
Family**	58	26
Friends**	50	19
Religious Leaders**	49	10
Teachers**	11	25
Youth Workers**	78	33
Nobody**	3	33

* Figures rounded to the nearest whole number.
** Statistically significant difference between the two groups (p<0.05)

Several of the youth clubs hosted small 'cell groups' which offered opportunities for Bible study, prayer and discussion. These enhanced frequent churchgoers' sense of belonging to a Christian community. Close relationships and emotional connection with group members was an important aspect of the cell group experience. Violet explained that her cell group is 'close and we're really all good friends'. The cell provides 'time to meet up and talk about stuff and church'. She found church services routine and boring, whereas in the cell group 'we get to talk ... about all the things that are going on at the moment'. Zoe said that her cell group made her feel more confident in her faith, 'and you're accountable to one another, so you can help each other and also you're gonna be stronger friends because you've got such ... an important thing [Christianity] as a foundation. Not just friendship.' Briony confirmed this. Cathy said, 'It's important to meet with Christians your age and people your age who go through similar things.'

Each person within the cell group found confirmation of their self and their faith through the group. Here the young people were involved in explicit identity work as they sought out what it meant for them to be Christian and to live a Christian life. Their descriptions of the cell groups as a means of supporting Christian identity accords with research elsewhere on young Christians active in the faith (Shepherd 2009). Group activities such as Christian camps or pilgrimages provide intense social and spiritual experiences which strengthen Christian identity and validate faith. In this respect, Hervieu-Léger makes some useful differentiations between four different ways that faith is socially validated. These are useful in understanding why some approaches within the youth group were more helpful than others at sustaining faith.

Validating faith

Put simply, Hervieu-Léger (2001) identifies four 'validation regimes'. Traditionally the Church as an institution 'confirmed the beliefs and practices of the faithful' (2001:169). Its specially ordained priests and qualified theologians held the authority to rule on the correct interpretation of tradition and truth, and it was up to everyone else to conform to what they said. This hierarchical regime Hervieu-Léger refers to as 'institutional validation'. While our young people might respect the views of a priest or religious leader, generally they rejected such institutional authority in determining truth or having any sway on what they themselves might choose to believe.

A second type of validation is 'communal validation'. This tends to apply to smaller more egalitarian groups which work out for themselves a coherent set of norms, values and relations to the world, and in so doing create their own interpretation of truth and tradition. While leaders may emerge in such groups, faith is validated by reference to the group as a whole. Sociologically, communal validation fits with the notion of tight-knit 'sects', but it could be argued that an attenuated form of communal validation can be seen to be in operation within the looser structure of the cell groups as young people collectively work out, with the help of their youth worker, what it means to be a young Christian in late modernity. Group norms develop and these become the main point of faith validation implicitly or explicitly.

A third type of validation is 'self-validation'. Here the individual constructs her own narrative of faith and is open to drawing inspiration from a number of different spiritual traditions. She determines for herself what counts as true belief and correct practice based on her personal sense of certitude, often derived as much from emotional experience as from thinking things through. Some of the infrequent churchgoers in our study had self-validated belief – they worked out their religious beliefs entirely on their own, and judged for themselves if their faith was 'true' according to whether it felt right for them.

Self-validated belief is potentially quite fragile, however, especially under difficult circumstances. It takes a certain degree of self-assurance to stand by beliefs which are worked out in isolation. When religious faith is most needed it helps to have the 'backup' of other believers. This is why, as Davie suggests, institutional validation and a return to church is so appealing at, say, times of death. There is a certain solidity to institution and tradition which, coupled with the sheer weight of symbolic presence, provides reassurance that the tenets of faith are true, even if that reassurance is short-lived. Communal validation also provides the reassurance of other believers. With self-validation there is no such backup and that makes belief unstable. Consequently Hervieu-Léger identifies another validation regime which periodically emerges for those outside of coherent religious groups which she calls 'mutual validation'. With mutual validation the individual still constructs her own faith narrative, but does so by actively sharing ideas, experiences and testimonies with other people. The individual is still her own determining point of validation. She is not subject to institutional or group say-so, but nevertheless gains security of faith by recognizing the authenticity of others' beliefs and, through social interaction, the authenticity of her own faith position.

Rather than seeing these regimes of validation as mutually exclusive 'types', we found it helpful to think of them as points on a continuum of strength of group validation: self-validation at one end, the least dependent on a group, moving into mutual validation, then communal and finally institutional validation at the other end which is dependent on the most established church organization. Faith is most readily transmitted where there is strong group validation (communal or institutional). Cell groups seemed to operate at the point where mutual validation tips over to communal validation. Worshipping together, journeying together and sharing personal testimonies were all vital for a sense of belonging and sustaining Christian identity. Some of the youth groups offered Alpha courses which also bridged from mutual to communal validation. In these cases, even if individuals were free to explore their own ideas within the context of the Alpha group, there was still an underlying Christian belief system which they were encouraged to edge towards.

However, most of the youth and community work projects in our study, in line with the ethos of informal education, tended to be more towards the mutual and self-validating end of the spectrum. Group discussions, for example, were arranged to enable young people to work out what they think about religious ideas without any influence from the youth workers. This, as we shall see, makes it more difficult for youth work to raise Christian consciousness (young people might not want to talk about religion) and to pass on the Christian memory (religion simply becomes a matter of personal conjecture).

Life and society

The second reason our infrequent churchgoers were mildly interested in Christianity was that they were aware that religion is still an important dimension of life in the late modern world for some people. Indeed, it would be hard for them to be unaware of the increasing salience of religion in the news media and popular culture. They were therefore interested in Christianity as part of their broader engagement with society. Gary, for example, said Christianity is 'relevant to society . . . 'cause you need religion for society'. Ariel told her youth worker Christianity 'has a major influence in life and society and therefore I'm interested, because it does have an impact'. Dean went into more detail. He explained that what interest he had stemmed from his observations that

> there are a lot of Christians around and I meet up with you lot [youth workers] and you're all Christians and I'm interested in that and why you're Christians. And we do go into the church buildings every week when we go to club . . . it's mainly a Christian country; so all these things make me a bit interested in Christianity. (Dean to youth worker)

Skye was interested in talking about Christianity because she liked exploring ideas about life:

> I'm kind of interested in Christianity but it's more because of the people – I enjoy talking about life more. Sometimes this means Christianity, especially when I come here [to club]. (Skye)

Bernadette made a similar point. She enjoyed 'deep, deep conversations' about where we come from and would talk to her friends and the Christian youth workers about it. 'Everyone loves that kind of talk' she said.

When it came to the role of religion in society and what beliefs and practices characterize different religions, school RE classes were the main contexts for learning. This included learning about Christianity. Mia, for example, had a 'reasonable interest in Christianity. I've gone to school where RE was taught. I was also Jesus in the school play.' Dylan thought Christianity was the most interesting religion from his RE classes and he would like to know more about it. On the other hand Jacqui had heard about Christianity 'over and over again' at school; 'I get fed up with it.'

The burden of proof

Some young people found the different perspectives offered by their school subjects hard to reconcile with faith. This was particularly the case in terms of perceived competing narratives of creation offered by science and the Bible.

> I don't know 'cause it's confusing; 'cause at school you can have RE about Adam and Eve, then we have to go to science and learn about evolution. So they contradict each other. (Grace)

> I don't know, I just – I'm kind of struggling more towards the Big Bang idea than being created. (Polly)

Faced with competing ideas the young people had to judge the truth claims of both sides which made school religion quite academic. Propositional beliefs tended to be judged in the first instance on the basis of objective 'evidence' or 'proof'. In this respect a 'technological consciousness' (see Chapter 1, Berger et al. 1974) was present among our young people.

Hayden said, 'nobody's seen any evidence of God's existence' and he would not believe until there is evidence there. Toby told his youth worker he would like to believe in God, but 'I've got no proof for myself, but I want proof'. Bernadette did not have enough proof to believe that 'we come out of a woman's left rib; one of them – right or left.' On the other hand Gary believed that Jesus had existed because there was 'proof that he had been born'. Cameron thought that God had shown himself in nature. Charlie said he believed in 'spiritual stuff' because 'something must have started this universe off, nature makes that obvious, don't you see'.

The urge for proof extended beyond religious beliefs for some young people. Jack and Iain, for example, enjoyed watching the television programme *Most Haunted* which purported to investigate the spirit world scientifically. They followed suit and tried to record ghosts on their mobile phones. Jack said, 'I woke up in the morning and you could hear "woosh", all the windows were closed and my phone was actually in a different position.'

The contingent nature of scientific evidence and theory, however, did not escape young people's imagination either. Thus, for Toby 'the "Big Bang" is just a theory' in his mind and 'the Bible has some valid stuff to say about creation'. Francis' survey of over 33,000 13 to 15 year olds in the 1990s also points to some of the limitations of science in young people's minds. Francis (2001:171) found that 48% of weekly church attenders believed that 'God made the world in six days and rested on the seventh'; so too did 20% of those who went to church only sometimes and 10% of those who never went to church. In our much smaller survey, 37% of infrequent churchgoers (and 62% of frequent churchgoers) either disagreed or strongly disagreed with the statement that 'one day everything will be explained by science'.

Pluralism – each to their own

Understanding religion in society meant being aware of the diversity of religious faiths that people hold. Some, but not all, of our young people had firsthand experience of a plurality of faiths in their neighbourhood. Otherwise RE classes contributed to young people's understanding of other world faiths. Alicia, for example, noted

> In school I do RS; we do religious studies. And we talk about Muslims, and
> they're saying that women should stay at home, look after their kids, bring
> them up as a Muslim, a good Muslim, pray to God. And husbands should go
> out to work and bring their kids up as good Muslims.

Finlay, however, thought that more time should be devoted to Christianity
within the curriculum because it is 'our own country's religion'. He told his
youth worker 'he did about one and half weeks on Christianity in RE and then
the rest of the time did Hinduism and stuff'. Karen concurred:

> I wasn't really interested in like religious studies. . . . I didn't really want to
> know about Muslims . . . I forgot the rest. Hindu, I wasn't interested really. It
> wasn't really my religion, that's probably why. But Christianity I was
> [interested in].

We saw in Chapter 1 that sociologists take different views of the effects of
pluralism on the maintenance and transmission of religion in society. Some
argue that it undermines the plausibility of faith since so many conflicting ideas
about the same thing suggests nobody has '*the* answer' so why bother with
any? Others argue that pluralism opens up a spiritual marketplace which caters
for everyone's spiritual needs and in finding satisfaction belief is sustained. The
tendency in our sample was for neither of these positions to be true. Our young
people were generally interested in what others believed and they liked to
discuss their own opinions when religion arose in conversation in the youth
club. Awareness of religious diversity did not cause them to reject religion but
nor for the most part did it prompt them to become proactive in searching
beyond their own religious inheritance.

The young people were universally keen to stress in the interviews that they
respected other people's beliefs and practices. Certainly as far as their
perception of the youth workers' faith was concerned the young people did not
mind what faith position they held. 'It's like they can be who they want to be,
and I can be who I want to be' (Ashley). 'I believe they can believe what they
want to. They can believe in Hindu or some Buddhist or something like that. It
won't change what I think about them' (Barry). Ike was happy for his youth
worker to be Christian 'if it's helping her'. This attitude of each to their own
fitted with a normative imperative of tolerance towards religions. To some
extent it also expressed the centrality of the authentic self as a cultural ideal
among young people; people should follow the beliefs that reflect and support
their true subjective self – this is what 'counts' above all else and therefore
should not be interfered with.

It could also be argued, of course, that tolerance is less about respect for others than indifference. It simply did not matter to our young people what somebody's religious faith was if they kept it to themselves and did not try to force it on others.[5] There are plenty of other areas where things *do* matter to young people where tolerance is less forthcoming. During one of the observed youth work sessions Cain, the youth worker, encouraged his group of young people to create a superhero and 'play God' with the world. The exercise drew attention to the separation between different groups of young people in the local area – 'the chavs versus the grungers, the middle class kids versus the estate kids'. Cain went on to work with these young people around issues of forgiveness and respect, and tolerance for others. Nevertheless as far as religion was concerned, and in the context of the youth club at least, the young people were happy to live and let live. They enjoyed finding out about others' ideas when the occasion arose and yet remained quite detached from those ideas in terms of their own sense of faith. Religious diversity and knowing that others think differently to oneself did not, therefore, undermine the potential for religious or spiritual beliefs, but it also did not provoke 'shopping' in the spiritual marketplace. Instead it provided a context in which the young person could rehearse and examine their own, otherwise implicit, existing ideas. In other words, the youth club for infrequent churchgoers tended to provide a context for mutual validation in Hervieu-Léger's terms.

Trilli illustrates the point. She was interested in spirituality and was pleased to talk about it in the youth group because 'there's so much out there you can't be wrong with it. Therefore my opinion counts, and the opinions of the people I'm talking to count. So there isn't a right or wrong answer'. Hilary thought that with religion 'there's no right or wrong answer, it is just your opinion isn't it, so'. Rachel said:

> Well, I don't think to defend my opinion but it is always good listening to other people's opinions. It's not necessarily changing your opinion, but you open your mind and possibly see other things. I'm not sure, but it's definitely great to listen to other people's opinions.

The result of mutual validation in the youth club was a self-referential loop which simply reinforced what individuals already thought. This was apparent in the style of conversations the young people had with the youth workers at the beginning and end of the study. The answers rarely changed; they just became more definite in one direction or another.

Guidelines for living

The third reason infrequent churchgoers gave for being moderately interested in Christianity was in terms of the guidelines it provided for living. The freedoms invoked by individualization bring pressures to bear on young people who are faced with having to make choices about how to live and what lifestyle to adopt. Such choices raise questions of ethics and morality, particularly in relation to matters of personal relationships and consumption. Should I sleep with my boyfriend? Is it OK to take drugs or get drunk? Although our young people were keen to assert their autonomy they were also looking for points of reference to help them in their decision-making. Family and friends were central in helping young people come to their own decisions, a point we come back to in Chapter 5.

Be good

Christianity as a religion was seen as one moral framework which they could refer to for general values and guidance on what a 'good life' might consist of. Julie put it like this: the 'Christian faith offers a good guideline to life and it helps people. It's not the faith that I'm interested in, it's the beliefs that that faith holds'. Charlie, who did not believe in a personal God, nevertheless saw Christianity as a 'good thing' which helps people. He thought of 'Jesus as a good man, he taught people how to live and taught people how to do the right thing and live the right way'. Leo thought the world was in a mess, but that 'if we were like Jesus there would be no problem'. James thought of Jesus as a 'good man; he cared, he was peaceful and he wanted things done properly'. By 'properly' James meant with justice. Finlay saw the 'church as a really positive place' because of 'all the good things that they do in the community'. The association of Christianity with being and doing good was therefore present among our young people, both infrequent as well as frequent churchgoers.

There was also a sense that Christianity implied a certain degree of personal restraint. For Alice this meant, among other things, no sex before marriage and no smoking. As an agnostic, she did not think the Church had any right to dictate such behaviours to her. However, she did feel that those who professed to be religious should live by the rules of their faith. 'If you say you follow something, why aren't you following it?' Not to do so was seen as hypocritical and as undermining authentic living. If religious people act hypocritically young people wonder what the point of religion actually is. In their mind religion should make a difference. This has implications for passing on faith to young people. Christian youth workers, leaders, parents, and congregations have to display the professed virtues of the faith at least as popularly understood – kindliness, love, forgiveness, charity etc. – if it is going to be taken seriously. While witnessing these virtues does not necessarily inspire young people to explore the Christian faith themselves, to display the opposite will certainly undermine the credibility of Christianity. In this respect our young people conformed to Davie's (2007a) view of vicarious religion, in that they expected churchgoers – including their Christian youth workers – to uphold high standards of moral behaviour. It is far easier to turn young people off religion than to turn them on to it by example.

It is to their credit that the youth workers in our study were held in high regard by the young people in their clubs. Indeed, they were often described as friends and in the case of one group of girls 'treated like family', which was the highest compliment they could give. Youth workers in this respect at least contributed to young people's immanent faith (Chapter 3). Some young people even saw a tenuous connection between the youth workers' faith and the youth worker's desire to work with young people. However, this in itself did not attract young people to explore the Christian faith any further. When asked what motivated the youth workers, Horace said 'the Bible innit, Christianity'. Polly said it was because they liked the 'kids' but 'also probably to do with their religion as well ... they like helping people'. Cathy thought the youth workers were motivated to help young people 'get through the Christian faith 'cos it's hard when you're teenagers'. One or two made the link with religious faith but understood in a rather different way. Wendy, for example, said that God motivates the youth workers; they 'want God to think they are doing something good maybe, and they'll go to heaven'. Sue added 'Karma. You do something good, you get something good back in return'. Clive saw religious motivation as secondary, 'helping change the environment, like making youth of today happy ... I mean even if youth of today don't want to get into God they are still having a fun place to like socialize and interact with other people'.

Beyond being and doing good, however, the link between a way of living, belief in God and its deeper connection to the Christian story was more or less absent. Youth workers tried to make the connection but the meaning sometimes got lost along the way, as was evident in a conversation between Bob, the interviewer, and two young people, Trisha and Zac.

> 'We were doing stuff downstairs with water and then we read the Bible with the water ...' Trisha told Bob. 'Tell me what happened' Bob replied. Trisha described the game: 'I had a big pan of water and we all had a spoon, and we had to take some water and try and carry it over to the bucket, and then had to pick it up.' 'And see how long it would take,' Zac chipped in. 'What was that, what did that prove?' Bob asked. 'I can't remember' said Zac. 'Oi, Kirsty!' he called across the room. 'What did that water thing have to do with?'

'What water?' Kirsty asked. 'When we had to use the spoons to fill the bucket, why did we do that? I can't remember.' 'Perseverance', said Kirsty, 'and because it was funny.'

Place

Alongside communities of learning several of the young people identified physical places as being triggers for a raised Christian consciousness. We have discussed the significance of place more fully elsewhere (Nash et al. 2007), but it is worth noting here that place is an important way in which the Christian memory has been transmitted through the centuries. Churches, cathedrals and shrines all communicate the on-going story of Christianity as each generation leaves its mark on the landscape. In this respect a distinction is usually drawn between 'place', which contains meanings, memories and identity, and 'space', which is empty of meaning. Spaces are non-places; empty halls, airport lounges, homogenized shopping malls are examples of spaces where actions are performed but the physical location is incidental. These spaces may, of course, become significant for individuals, and when they do, they become places.

Although the infrequent churchgoers rarely went to church services, several of them indicated that church buildings had become meaningful places to them in their connection with their own personal biography or family narratives (baptisms, weddings and funerals being some obvious examples). Some also recalled how, on the rare occasions they had been in church, they had been prompted to think about God. Alicia, for example, said:

> There was a church I went in and there was like all angels up, if you look . . . I can't explain them. You've got the cross and Jesus on it and you look at that and just think, I can't really explain it. It's just a feeling. That was when I was little though.

Two of our young people recalled how they used to visit the grounds of a church with their friends; their relationship to the building was interesting because whatever else they might do there, they also prayed in the church when invited to do so by the priest:

Interviewer:	One last thing, how often do you go to church, of your own free will?
Iain:	Er
nterviewer:	Never?

Jack:	Sometimes we used to. Not like – the church wasn't open – but we used to go to church. And there's a bit of a hallway you have to go in there . . .
Iain:	Oh yeah.
Jack:	. . . and you have to pray.
Iain:	Yeah.
Interviewer:	Oh you did that, on your own?
Jack:	We used to do that.
Interviewer:	You and your friends?
Jack:	Yeah, he [Larry] used to come as well, and another guy called Malcolm.
Interviewer:	Oh that's interesting, why did you do that?
Jack:	Because we knew it was open and we spoke to the priest and he said 'Come in and pray'.
Iain:	'Come in whenever you want'.
Jack:	Yeah.

Storied vs unstoried places

In Jack and Iain's case, the cultural understanding of place and building evoked action. That a cultural memory still exists of church buildings as special places was evidenced in two other conversations with young people whose youth club met inside a church. One found it 'weird' that a youth club was housed in the church – he expected it to be held in something more like a pavilion. Another young person said the church building made her feel 'safe'. These descriptions of 'weird' and 'safe' suggest these young people connected church buildings with particular sorts of activities – worship and prayer – and sanctuary.

Insofar as the young people could bring an understanding of the Christian tradition to a place they could begin to know what to do in it – spaces became storied places. In contrast, some of the youth clubs in ordinary buildings had prayer rooms which had been fitted out to be comfortable, quiet places, but which carried none of the immediate cues associated with places of prayer. Addie, who had little sense of the Christian tradition, approached her club's prayer room as space, an 'unstoried place', and consequently used it to relax rather than pray. Similarly, Matt reported that the infrequent churchgoers who took part in a labyrinth prayer exercise around a modern church building tended to treat it more as a relaxing exercise, somewhere to gather thoughts rather than pray. Matt (the youth worker) explained that the church itself carried few cues to the Christian memory:

> It doesn't look much like a church, it just looks like a big room . . . And we do all kinds of things in there as well. We clear the pews and we play games, and we sort of run around. You know, all kinds of stuff really. So it's not treated maybe in a traditional way as a sacred space.

In the absence of the Christian story, the young people did not always know what to do with opportunities for religious engagement, so they simply relaxed and reflected upon their selves and their lives.

Fading memory

From the above we are able to conclude two things about the role of Christian youth work in raising Christian consciousness and maintaining the Christian memory, the original question underlying our research. First, for frequent churchgoers, the Christian youth work raises Christian consciousness and nurtures Christian faith. It is a vital source of support for young Christians, helping them to explore their faith and maintain their Christian identity. Second, for infrequent churchgoers, though the youth work did occasionally raise their Christian consciousness, in most instances it did not engender a deepening interest in Christianity since the processes of mutual validation supported young people's self-discovery of religious truth rather than the discovery of the Christian story and tradition. That said, the youth work did keep the plausibility and *possibility* of Christian faith alive for infrequent churchgoers. Youth workers held the faith to which the young people could vicariously refer should they need to. They laid the traces of ritual through prayer and, in some cases, worship. They demonstrated the plausibility of faith by themselves believing. They upheld Christian virtues and they provided opportunities for the young people to think about moral and ethical issues in the context of a Christian framework. The latter takes us to Chapter 5.

5

A good life

So far we have considered the nature of young people's faith and its relationship to Christianity (Chapter 3), and the transmission of faith in terms of passing on the Christian memory (Chapter 4). In this final empirical chapter we are faced with the 'so what' question. What are the implications of the Christian faith for how young people choose to live their lives? We have seen that faith in God can be important to get through difficult times but does this faith also impact on day-to-day decisions? Young people sometimes see the potential of Christianity for providing guidelines to live by but what do they understand those guidelines to be and to what extent do they refer to them? These are questions to do with the ethical outworking of faith and what makes for a 'good life'.

From Aristotle to youth clubs

What constitutes a good life has been an important feature of popular and political debate over the last few years. To give just two examples, Prof. Michael Sandel in the 2009 Reith lectures called for a public discourse over what might constitute a new politics of the common good that would engage with moral and spiritual questions. Around the same time, the Children's Society launched its report, *A Good Childhood: Searching for Values in a Competitive Age* (Layard and Dunn 2009). More than 30,000 children, adults and professionals contributed to that inquiry. The report argued that the greatest threat to children's welfare comes from the aggressive pursuit of personal success by adults believing that the prime duty of the individual is to make the most of their own life rather than contribute to the good of others.

Though the idea of a good life may have become prominent in public discourse fairly recently, it is hardly a new concept. It derives from Aristotle's *Nicomachean Ethics*. Stanley Hauerwas (1981a), Alastair MacIntyre (1985) and Charles Taylor (1991) are all a part of what is sometimes called the 'neo-Aristotelian revival', a school of thought that sees ethical behaviour as being decided by one's understanding of what makes for a good life, which in turn is decided by the primary community of which one is a part. An individual fulfils his purpose by living a good life however that is defined by the community. Family, school, peer groups, church for those who went and, of course, youth clubs were the different communities which shaped our young people's understanding of ethical living. Each community had a different sense of how to live a good life. The church suggested faithful living, schools laid down rules, the youth club created a moral space where issues could be discussed, peers gave opinions on the right thing to do, family created a basic moral framework. For our infrequent churchgoers, however, none of these communities provided an ethical framework adequate to the complexity of some of the situations they faced. For infrequent churchgoers Christian values were vaguely in the background of social understandings of morality but belief in God (howsoever conceived) had little relevance to their decision-making. Family and friends were key points of reference but young people's primary ethical tool was themselves with authenticity, 'being true to oneself', as the guiding principle. Ultimately the young people end up with a self-directed code of ethics relying largely on their own intuitions, feelings and experience. Our young people therefore tended to be quite pragmatic and self-reliant in their approach to living.

A good life can be linked to having a sense of purpose and churchgoers are likely to have a stronger sense of life purpose than non-churchgoers because they have a strong community of which they feel a part and which regularly articulates its understandings of how to live a good life through its preaching and teaching. Our research suggests that this is true for young people; so too does Francis (2001). His Teenage Religion and Values survey found that 70% of 13 to 15 year olds who went to church weekly had a sense of purpose compared to 59% who went to church sometimes and 49% who never went to church. Similarly 73% of weekly churchgoers said that they find life really worth living, compared to 70% of those who were occasional churchgoers and 68% of non-churchgoers (2001:168). A break in the lineage of believers – the community of faith – does not just mean a loss of religious knowledge and understanding, but also potentially a loss of purpose. In our previous research we looked at the worldview young people shared among their peer community and found in that an understanding that the aim of life was to be 'happy' (Savage et al. 2006:38). Happiness was to be achieved through young people 'being themselves' and being in good relationships with others. This constituted the implicit work-a-day world view of the 'happy midi-narrative' (see Chapter 1) and it was echoed by the young people in our current study when we asked them what they thought was most important in life. As we saw in Chapter 3 family and friends were central to immanent faith – 'never forget your family, it's always on the top of your list'. Being happy and realizing individual potential was also important. For Martin, speaking to his youth worker, the most important thing in life is

> socializing with you guys, be happy with yourself, be happy with what you're given and try not to have big regrets, and just whatever comes your way try to be happy with it.

We wondered whether our infrequent churchgoing young people could add anything else to this view if they were asked about their sense of purpose more directly. The happy midi-narrative need not exclude other ways of thinking about the world and the youth club may have raised their Christian consciousness to explore a sense of purpose in relation to God. We therefore asked our infrequent churchgoers in Phase 2 whether they thought their life had an *ultimate* purpose.

Plans rather than purpose

Overall our young people were moderately sure that their lives did have an ultimate purpose though some were more convinced than others. Mia, for example, thought that there was no point living without purpose – 'you may as well die'. Thomas said, 'everyone's got to have a reason to live'. Sienna thought that 'we've been put on earth for some reason . . . If we weren't there wouldn't be any point to anything'. Bradley concurred: there must be a purpose 'otherwise what's the point?' What that point might actually be, however, was elusive. Emma and Maisie echoed Jacqui's thought that 'we must be here for something, but I'm not really sure what it is'. Maisie went on to venture a guess that in her case it might be 'to make other people feel good'; others suggested helping people. Some of the young people thought that they would find their purpose during the course of their lives, or even at the end of their life when they looked backed and saw how it all fitted together (Emma).

Not being entirely sure of their ultimate purpose did not seem to cause the young people too many problems. In the same way that the young people were happy to pray believing in the possibility of God rather than necessarily needing to believe that God actually existed (Chapter 3), so in terms of purpose assuming that there was one appeared to be good enough for daily living without being overly concerned as to what that ultimate purpose actually might be. To have a sense of ultimate purpose may make them 'feel alive' (Sienna) or 'whole and complete' (Bradley) if they had one, but otherwise they just got on with the business of living. 'I go to work, come home, that's it, that's my life,' said Letitia. She went on to tell her youth worker that

> She was quite happy as she was, and it didn't bother her at all that she didn't have a sense of purpose. She was just kind of taking each day as it came and dealing with that as it came. (Lucy, youth worker)

Indeed, Dean was quite relieved *not* to have a sense of what his ultimate purpose was as he felt that would put him under too much pressure. Others thought that you have to create your own purpose by making the most of life. As Julie put it, 'you live and then die. You've just got to make the most of what you've got.' Charlie put it more strongly: 'I want to be in control of my own life. I don't like the idea that somebody else tells me what to do. I don't believe in it.'

Although our young people did not need to know their ultimate purpose they did usually have *plans*. Plans replaced purpose. When asked what she thought the purpose of her life was, Amanda replied, 'I don't really think in that way. I just think what can I be to make my life have more meaning.' There was often a conventional and understated sense of ambition in the plans they described. Evie said her purpose was 'having a big house, getting married, having children and getting a good job'. For Kian too it was 'get a good job and have children'. There was a common recognition that they needed to prepare themselves and work hard to realize their plans. When asked what he wanted to achieve in life Jason thought first of education and then career related goals. Zac said the most important thing in life was getting good grades in his GCSEs and exams. Hilary wanted to 'keep her head up, work hard and be really successful'. Nancy and Olivia said that they would work hard for what they wanted even though they did not know what that was at the moment. There was a streak of realism, even sensibleness in these attitudes that belies the assumption that teenagers are rebelling against a tight parental structure. James thought it was important to 'pay taxes to make the country work'. Finlay's reflection on growing up was that 'you expect to rebel against your parents. And then when you get older you turn into your parents, so you do'. In fact one or two of the young people saw their parents as anti-role models giving them an example of what *not* to do. They did not want to make the same mistakes their parents had. Emma talked about wanting to work at not being like her Mum who had left school with no qualifications, had her child early and then divorced. Looking back at her life during an activity in the youth club, Emma realized she wanted to work hard at school so life would be different and better.

The fact that the young people were more able to talk about plans rather than purpose was indicative of the fact religious narratives were not a strong feature in how they approached their day-to-day living. They were not thinking about the purpose of life in broad terms nor thinking about vocations or callings. They generally saw it as their responsibility to work out what they wanted to do with their lives and how to go about achieving those goals. The youth workers tried to encourage the young people to think about purpose in their lives but as with other aspects of raising Christian consciousness, it tended to be the frequent churchgoers who engaged with the religious element in these interventions rather than the infrequent churchgoers. 54% of frequent churchgoers compared to 28% of infrequent churchgoers said that the youth club helped them think of the purpose of life. Elliot was a frequent churchgoer who had engaged with the question of purpose. The religious language in reply to the question 'what was most important to him?' was evident:

> Well, I've had a change of heart recently because I've just sort of been challenged about being a 'living sacrifice'. So, loving God and loving other people I suppose. But obviously like my own priorities come first as well.

What would a 'normal headed' person do?

Realizing one's plans for life involves making right choices along the way. It was clear that our young people did have a sense of things being good and bad, right and wrong – and they aimed to choose the 'right' and the 'good'. As we saw in Chapter 3, shame and guilt were occasionally confessed in private prayers and forgiveness sought. It was one of the attractions of Christianity for some of our infrequent churchgoers as well as our frequent churchgoers that it potentially provided guidelines for living (Chapter 4) and could help the young people make right choices. Just what these guidelines might be beyond being a helpful and caring person was unclear from the young people's comments. The closest mention our infrequent churchgoers made to guidelines was the ten commandments in terms of 'thou shalt not kill' and 'thou shalt not steal'. Trilli, for example, explained to her youth worker that she liked Christian values and said that the ten commandments 'helps us all live better lives', and that this affected her decisions 'because I'm not gonna go and kill somebody'. Cameron remembered being in the Boys' Brigade when he was younger (7 or 8 years old) and he had wanted to steal some chocolate. He explained to his youth worker he was 'going to do it but then "thou shalt not steal" kind of popped into his head' so he did not take it. Bradley thought that laws are based on the Bible and the ten commandments, 'well I wouldn't break any of those' he said. However, his motivation for keeping the ten commandments was not so much 'what would Jesus do', he said, but rather 'I would say with me it was just kind of "what would a 'normal headed' person do?" Would I get arrested?'

In Phase 2 we asked the young people whether their decisions were influenced by their beliefs about, and awareness of, God since in Phase 1 45% of the infrequent churchgoers said that they believed in some sort of God and a third agreed with the statement that 'God is important to me'. Clive was one of the few infrequent churchgoers who said that believing in God had influenced his lifestyle: it caused him to stop taking drugs with his friends. On the whole, however, God did not come into infrequent churchgoers' decision-making. Charlie said, 'we just make our own mind up, we just do what we think. God's not interested in us, we just carry on anyway.' Benjamin said his decisions are not based on beliefs about God at all, but rather on 'possible outcomes, repercussions'. Barry was asked whether his belief in reincarnation affected how he lived his life. He said, 'Not really no. I just act myself and do what I would do normally. I wouldn't be bad, I wouldn't be good, I'd be just myself.'

Youth club as moral community

The fact that the young people were interested in having Christian guidelines for living but had only a vague awareness of what they might be suggests the loss of Christian memory also means a loss of an ethical framework. This does not mean that it cannot be replaced – the Church does not hold a monopoly on moral interpretation – but it does mean that one ethical resource is denied to those who are not part of a faith community. Davie's description of vicarious religion (2007a, see Chapter 1) implies that society needs this ethical resource. She holds out a tentative suggestion that the English population takes an interest in Church debates concerning moral issues because it is a way for society in general to consider what it thinks, and on what basis it holds its opinions. For our young people a lack of clear guidelines meant that they were thrown back on their own resources and had to become serious moral thinkers in their own right. Bessie illustrates the point:

> It's on your mind every day really isn't it. You come across situations where you need the right thing and the wrong thing to do, but sometimes you make the wrong decision and sometimes you think, 'Ahh, what would happen if I would have done the wrong thing or the right thing.' So one big headache!

The youth club was one community which helped the young people to develop their ethical thinking by providing them with an important moral space where they could discuss matters of right and wrong as these applied to their own lives. Both the infrequent and frequent churchgoers recognized that the youth work had developed their thinking in this way.

In this respect the youth workers helped the young people to build up their inner resources to deal with the situations that confronted them, both in terms of hypothetical 'what to do if ...' type of discussions and more immediate practical advice concerning different situations. Colin mentioned some of the themes he had discussed in his youth group: 'they have stuff about God, sometimes they'd be about love, teenage stuff, animal cruelty, whatever'.

Other times the guidance on what to do was more personal. Addie was off school for a long time and was encouraged by the youth worker to go back. Karen described her youth worker as helping her decide what she wanted to do in the future. Lois was helped to come to terms with an eating disorder. She commented as follows:

> When I'm here I don't feel people are judging me ... here they were giving me some slack and they didn't 'diss' me. They were talking to me like I was an adult ... saying you're worth more than this. Like, when I was a child I was being the big one out of my family and I was, like, looking at TV and magazines and it was all slim, pretty girls that got the boys.

Nancy explained how the youth worker had helped her to cope with her father.

> When my dad was hitting me, I didn't have anyone to go to talk about this. And then Freda [youth worker] comes, she helped me through it. And she tells me whenever me dad starts, just walk away and just go upstairs in my room, or go out. And now every time my dad starts I walk away, I go out, I don't come back until later on that night.

However, while the young people were happy to receive advice, they were clear that they did not want to be told what to do or think. They sometimes contrasted this with school which they found more restrictive in terms of moral thinking. Cecilia explained that the youth workers offer guidelines on things like drugs: 'I wouldn't say they were rules or like telling us what to do, you take it or leave it.' She went on to say that the youth workers were more like counsellors and friends. Alicia agreed that the youth workers were 'on the level. They're not like school teachers.' Trilli indicated that for her RE class was a 'waste of time' in terms of moral thinking, because 'they just tell you what to do. . . . It's like when we did abortions we were told that it's all wrong, wrong, wrong, wrong and there was no options.' Kay and Francis (1996:56) note that closing down discussion in a religious education context tends to contribute towards young people holding negative attitudes towards Christianity.

Another important influence on young people's learning about right and wrong came from the rules of the club. Obviously there were times when unacceptable behaviour in the club was corrected. But more than this: the young people themselves recognized the value of the club's rules and took ownership of them themselves. Here again several of the young people, like Hilary, contrasted rules in the youth club with rules in school:

> There's a lot of rules in this club, but they're not rules like school rules or anything. They're rules that are easy to follow because it's obvious. It's easy to know what's right or wrong. But you don't really have a problem with the rules here because basically the rules are respect each other and just respect your elders and help each other and stuff like that.

Ownership of rules was most apparent when the young people gave examples of respecting the rules of the club. Barry even chose not to invite his friends to the club because

> they'd just hang around outside and ... they would be breaking the rules, doing stuff to the Centre and I just don't want that to happen, 'cos I know what they are like and I want to keep this place special.

The young people therefore recognized that rules were necessary for the smooth running of the club and that they benefitted from them. By imbibing the club rules in this way the young people implicitly took on something of the Christian culture, although they were not necessarily aware of doing so.

In upholding the rules of the club rather than conforming to peer pressures the young people were in the process of negotiating the varying moral expectations of the different communities of which they were a part. The clearest example of this came from Alice and Letitia who, as well as being members of their own youth club were also young leaders for a club for younger girls. The youth worker spent a lot of time working through the implications of being a youth leader in terms of Alice and Letitia's patterns of behaviour within the neighbourhood where they lived.

> ... so they've been kind of asking us questions like 'so does that mean then that if I go out and get drunk I get the taxi to drop me off at the back door, so the girls don't see me?' (Lucy, youth worker)

Alice and Letitia were struggling to reconcile their moral responsibilities with personal lifestyles, which were 'completely embedded in [the local] urban culture'. However, Alice indicated that she was trying to make decisions, not just for herself but for the younger girls as well, and she felt good about that.

Lost childhood of Generation Y

Though the youth club went some way to acting as an ethical community for the young people, it was the family (including the extended family) and friends which provided the primary communities to which they felt they belonged (Table 5.1). Families socialize their children into attitudes towards right and wrong, good and bad, moral obligation, duties and values, and remain a continuing point of reference. Friends helped to develop these ideas and work them out in practice. 'You know what's right and wrong when you're little' (Ike). Letitia told her youth worker her 'mum said the worst thing to do was lie. So she always thought she shouldn't lie'.

Managers and negotiators

The young people took their ethical cues from their parents, but their parents sometimes provided them with the most tricky ethical dilemmas they had to face. The Good Childhood Inquiry said that conflict in families that stay together can be more damaging than a well managed separation (Layard and Dunn 2009:23). Resilience is an invaluable emotional resource in helping children through difficult times. Debbie, for example, said that she lived with her mother until she was six and that when she was 16 she would go back and live with her again.

Our young people reported different types of relationships with parents. At one extreme they talked about parents as friends, at the other they spoke of absent parents. Ironically both extremes, for different reasons, had the same effect of seeing the young person move into an adult world at an early stage. Friendship parenting (see Chapter 3), though well intentioned, ran the risk that parents ended up competing for the same emotional space as their children's peers. One of the youth workers reflecting on our findings in the last stages of the research brings the point home. She notes that she regularly sees

Table 5.1 Who helps you make important decisions in your life?

	Frequent churchgoers* % agree	Infrequent churchgoers* % agree
Family	80	79
Friends	75	68
Youth workers**	47	18
Teachers	24	16

* Figures rounded to the nearest whole number.
** Statistically significant difference between the groups (p<0.05)

> an element of dysfunctionality in many of the young people's relations with parents. It's a different type to the ones of my generation (i.e. a power struggle, 'I hate you!' because I don't get my own way type arguments) . . . Instead what I've observed, at least in a few young people, is that this 'best friend' relationship with their mums can become highly volatile and emotionally strained. A bit like two young people in a playground being best friends, falling out and then making up again . . . So I do often find young people who want to distance themselves from parents but not in the same way or for the same reasons my generation did.

The result was that young people understood from an early age what it meant when things went wrong – particularly around broken relationships and divorce and the young people had to grow up fast. The young people ended up as negotiators, arbitrating between parents, adept or otherwise at managing change. Debbie appeared to be entirely practical about the need to make her restructured family unit work. Cecilia was quite willing to confide in and build relationships with the new members of her 'blended' family. There were two hidden effects of parental separation. One was a closer relationship with the parent (generally the mother) who had become the main carer. The second was the emotional pragmatism needed to adjust to the new situation. Neither Debbie nor Cecilia were sitting around waiting for their parents to get together again but were learning first to survive and then to thrive in their new environment.

Beck-Gernsheim (2002:18, 24, 7) talks about the normalization of fragility for the family. The breakdown of one set of relationships is not leading to the death of the family but to its reorganization (Drane and Fleming Drane 2004:32). Dennis was a case in point. He said that he neither saw his father nor even knew where he was living. Yet he still said that what he liked most about his family was that 'we are always there for each other when in need'; in this instance the family to which he referred was made up of his mother, step-father and sister.

Withers and Sheldon (2008) found that the young people's life online also confronted them with adult ethical issues. It created a parallel world of internet adulthood sophistication. They found that young people's use of the internet is often unsupervised and that many report being online for several hours a night using instant messaging and social networking sites, and that phones tend to be constantly on to avoid missing a text. They conclude that young people's technical expertise is greater than their understanding of the issues and risks associated with their online use and constant connectivity, and that there are implications for young people's well-being and possibly their psycho-social development. Mayo and Nairn (2009) say that children spend an average of five hours and 18 minutes a day in front of a screen – which, averaged over the course of a year, is more than double the time spent in class and one-and-a-half times that spent with parents; they conclude their study with the words 'Welcome to the war on children'.

In sum, our young people had to engage with adult issues before necessarily having the moral grounding so to do. Close relationships with significant adults and family members kick started young people's entrance into an adult world. This has left a generation capable but brittle and is what we are describing as the lost childhood of Generation Y.

Authenticity – the guiding principle

Evie and James were two young people interviewed in different parts of the country. They had never met, nor were they likely to do so, but essentially they said the same thing about how the decisions they made would come from them alone, authenticity was their guiding principle. Evie said, 'I'd make decisions myself and my family might help but they wouldn't make decisions for me ... I'm going to be a big woman and make my own decisions'. James was adamant that he was 'influenced by his own thoughts'. He said, 'nothing else outside has any effect on how I make decisions'.

We discussed in Chapter 1 the importance of individualization in late modern society. Duncan and Philips (2008) argue that individuals are condemned to chose their own biographies. The project of self with an emphasis on individual self-fulfilment and personal well-being replaces collective aims. Iain said, 'Get as much out it [life] as you can'. The young people's life chances were shaped by their ability to carve out opportunities for themselves. Margo et al. (2006) reckoned that personal and social skills became 33 times more important in shaping life chances between children born in 1958 and those born in 1970.

Authenticity is as much a pragmatic necessity as it is a moral ideal. However, the need for self-directed ethics did not translate into a selfish life. Beck's notion of 'altrustic individualism' was apparent (Beck & Beck-Gernsheim 2002:28). Finlay was clear that you could not just make decisions for yourself, you had to take other people into consideration, people like family and friends. Alice had a strong ethic about doing things for other people; she liked to make sure other people were OK, not just herself – this was so almost to the point of making sure others are OK before herself.

Finding our own authenticity leads to what Taylor (1991) sees as the 'good life'. The paradox is that we only become capable of understanding ourselves through our relationship with others. We define our identity through 'dialogue' with others. Taylor is a communitarian: authenticity and mutuality are dependent on each other. Authenticity implies both society and a common framework of ethics: 'in the culture of authenticity relationships are seen as the key loci of self-discovery and self-confirmation' (1991:49). Individualism as a moral principle must offer some view on how the individual should live with others in society.

Jack said the most important thing in life was to 'live life to the full but also to take care of things around you'. Taking care of others around you related to action. Alice wanted to help others. She said, 'All my friends turn to me for advice and counsel and that's what I am good at.' Chloe told her youth worker she wanted to be a 'child carer, work in a proper nursery and one day take it over'. Robert said that he gave money to charity to help poor people and 'to give other people a chance in their lives'. Our future, it appears, is in good hands.

Ethics, the new spirituality?

Overall it seems that for our infrequent churchgoing young people, just as they were getting by with a vague set of Christian beliefs for managing crises in their lives, so they were getting by with only a vague sense of Christian ethics. Daily decision making was located in immanent faith – especially the authentic self – with only loose connections to the Christian memory. However, it was also clear that the young people were at least implicitly aware of the need to develop the skills of ethical thinking as they worked through some of the complex issues in their lives. It is interesting to note in this respect that there has been an increasing number of young people enrolling in religious education courses at A level in recent years. The fact that the RE curriculum contains a large section on ethics is significant. Young people do not want to be told what to do, but they do want to know how to think and make right choices for themselves. Maybe ethics is the new spirituality. The Church has the potential to help them out.

6

Drawing the sociological strands together

At the beginning of this book we set out three questions we wanted to address in the course of our sociological investigation into young people's everyday faith:

1. What interest do young people have in Christianity?

2. How do social influences inform young people's Christian consciousness, especially faith-based youth and community work?

3. Does belief in God or a Christian identity make any difference to how young people live their lives?

Our focus has been particularly on young people who are infrequent churchgoers but who have contact with the Church through faith-based youth and community work. By infrequent churchgoers we mean young people who go to church less than once a month, if ever. They may have had a Christian upbringing and consider themselves nominally Christian, or they may have had no religious upbringing or have no sense of religious identity at all. The majority of young people in England can be described as infrequent churchgoers in this sense, and it is primarily through its youth and community work that the Church hopes to engage with them and interest them in the Christian faith. At various points throughout our discussion we have contrasted infrequent churchgoers with those young people in our sample who went to church more frequently (at least once a month) and who have a stronger sense of Christian identity. Chapters 3, 4 and 5 have set out our findings in detail, but before moving on to our theological reflections and considering the implications of our research for future mission and outreach, it may be helpful to summarize some of the key points so far.

What interest do young people have in Christianity?

All the major survey data outlined in Chapter 1 point to the fact that young people in England have generally disengaged from the Church and Christianity. Compared to previous generations, Generation Y young people are less likely to identify themselves as Christian, less likely to go to church, less likely to hold traditional Christian beliefs. Indeed, the everyday faith of the majority of young people tends not to be of a religious nature at all. Rather, it is invested in family, friends and the reflexive self. For the most part, family, friends and self are the central axes of meaning, hope and purpose which enables young people to get on with the business of daily living. We have called this 'immanent faith'.

That said, the rate of Christian decline appears to be beginning to 'bottom-out' and whilst most young people are indifferent to it, there remains a faint cultural memory of Christianity which they can, and to some extent do, access should they need to. This memory is kept alive partly through the continued structural relationships between Church and state in England, but mainly though the religious practices of a relatively small, active minority of Christians, some of whom are young people themselves. In this respect we found Grace Davie's concept of 'vicarious religion' helpful in thinking about young people's relationship to Christianity. To recap on Chapter 1, Davie defines vicarious religion as

> religion performed by an active minority but on behalf of a much larger number, who (implicitly at least) not only understand, but, quite clearly, approve of what the minority is doing (2007a:22).

Our 'active minority' of young people (the frequent churchgoers) may not have had a sense of performing faith for others. In fact, in keeping with the modern trend towards individualization, their engagement with Christianity tended to focus upon subjective experience and their own personal, friendship-oriented, relationships with God and fellow Christians. Nevertheless, they did keep the Christian memory going, and others from the wider community of faith (youth workers being our particular focus) were holding the faith for the majority infrequent churchgoers as well as for themselves. The infrequent churchgoers had an implicit understanding and approval of this insofar as on the odd occasions they needed religion it was the Christian tradition to which they usually turned. The clearest example of this was 'bedroom spirituality'. When they were alone at night many of our infrequent churchgoing young people prayed, adopting a practice which was loosely based on their knowledge of Christian prayer. They were most likely to pray in times of difficulty when immanent faith was not enough or was itself under threat (for example, through the illness of a parent or friend). In the absence of anything else, young people made do with their understanding of Christian beliefs and practices to keep hope alive. When the crisis was over, these beliefs and practices faded into the background and immanent faith once again came to the fore. Young people also occasionally used prayers in a process of self-reflection which included elements of confession and thanksgiving. Furthermore, when it came to rites of passage (birth, marriage and death) the young people joined in the Christian ceremonies appropriated by their families as part of the wider cultural tendency towards a vicarious relationship with Christianity.

Davie suggests that as well as making occasional use of the Church and Christian practices, vicarious religion manifests itself around expectations towards church leaders and churchgoers both in terms of belief and behaviour. Our infrequent churchgoers held some of these expectations too. They knew their youth workers were Christian and had Christian beliefs, and they were happy that this was the case. Our young people showed no hostility to Christianity in this respect. In their eyes it was a case of each to their own. Knowing that the youth workers were Christian meant that the fact that they prayed at the start of meetings or occasionally spoke about their faith was fine because it was simply a case of youth workers 'being themselves'. Authenticity was important to the young people whether it be in their own lives or the lives of other people. Similarly in terms of actions, the young people expected the youth leaders to act according to culturally recognized Christian principles such as kindliness, care, love and forgiveness. Fortunately the youth workers seem to have lived up to these expectations. However, some of the young people were aware of other Christians who had not and these they regarded as hypocrites. The profession of Christian faith should make a real difference to how one lives as far as our young people were concerned.

The last manifestation of vicarious religion, Davie tentatively suggests, is that the Church provides a space in which unresolved ethical issues can be debated and thereby vicariously resolved by wider society. For our young people faced with all the choices that accompany late modern individualism, how to live a good life was a pressing issue. In this respect young people were interested in Christianity in terms of the guidelines it could provide for living, and were keen to engage directly in debates within the youth clubs around ethical and moral issues.

In various ways then, the notion of vicarious religion illuminated some of our infrequent churchgoers' interest in Christianity.

How do social influences inform young people's Christian consciousness?

One of the reasons the Christian memory is faint is because many of the traditional mechanisms for transmitting faith have disappeared. We saw in Chapter 1 through the work of Danièle Hervieu-Léger that the best way to pass religion on is through participation in an actively believing community which rehearses the beliefs, practices and traditions of faith, retelling the stories of the past, interpreting their meaning and validating faith in the present for each new generation. In early modern times kinship relations, work and leisure, local community, belief and tradition all came together in the parish system to maintain the Christian faith. Under the forces of modernization this arrangement broke down; religion can no longer be taken for granted and the form faith takes becomes a matter of individual choice.

Our infrequent churchgoers were, by definition, not part of church communities and therefore not best placed to inherit the Christian faith in all its fullness. Few, however, were completely unchurched. Many had been taken to church when they were younger. Some had gone to Sunday School, others took part in Christmas services or attended occasional services for family events. A few had learnt about Christianity through discussion with family and friends at home; often in these cases it fell to grandparents to introduce children to the faith since parents were either uninterested or reluctant to impose religion on their children. In this respect there was little evidence of rebellion against parental beliefs amongst our young people because there was usually very little to rebel against. 'Benign indifference' was the best description of our infrequent churchgoers' attitude towards Christianity.

Schools also had given many of our young people at least some church experience through things like school Masses, harvest festivals, nativity plays, end of term assemblies and so on. These sorts of activities had given the young people a feel for Christian practices, in particular prayer, which formed the foundation for the expression of bedroom spirituality and reflection mentioned above. Religious education lessons were the young people's primary source of information about Christianity and other world religions, though these lessons were not intended to encourage any particular faith as such, and their knowledge of Christianity was at best abstract and patchy. The young people indicated that grappling with the truth claims of religion *vis à vis* science in the classroom often left them unsure about what to believe. This uncertainty did not seem to bother many of our infrequent churchgoers; they were prepared to live with the uncertainty as religion was not that important to them. The exception to this was around death and the afterlife.

Our young people expressed an interest in wanting to make clearer sense of these.

The Christian youth and community work projects our young people participated in were often the closest they came to a believing community. The youth workers provided different opportunities in their activities for young people to think about the Christian faith and engage with its practices. These included amongst other things, the provision of prayer spaces, the display of religious symbols and artefacts, time for discussion, activities with a Christian message or going away to Christian youth camps. The infrequent churchgoers were aware of the Christian ethos of the group and respected its rules and the youth workers' faith which sustained it. Indeed, the very fact that the youth workers, as respected adults, were known to be Christian helped to maintain the plausibility of the faith for some. Most, however, did not come to the group for religious reasons, they came to socialize with friends and have fun. Consequently the youth workers were keen to ensure that any attempts to raise young people's Christian consciousness was not experienced as imposed and fitted with the informal education approach of this type of youth work. The young people appreciated the fact that religion was not forced upon them and sometimes voluntarily took advantage of the opportunities for religious reflection. They enjoyed discussing ideas and hearing about other people's beliefs. In so doing infrequent churchgoers entered into a process of mutual validation whereby each individual had their subjective beliefs confirmed by everyone else, whatever those beliefs might be. This was good for helping young people clarify their ideas, but on the whole failed to transmit Christian faith to them beyond what they had held prior to the group. Moreover, there was little evidence of our young people shopping around the spiritual market for different ideas. The infrequent churchgoers tended to respond to, rather than initiate, opportunities for religious engagement in the group. Most of our young people thought of religion and spirituality as the same thing and tended to conceive of this as being the faith tradition they were brought up in.

The picture was different for frequent churchgoers' engagement with the Christian youth groups. These young people were very keen to explore their faith with other Christians and appreciated the support and communal validation they gained from the youth and community work, especially when youth workers set up 'cell groups' where the exploration of faith was more direct and deliberate. Indeed, this support made up for a lack of involvement the young people sometimes felt in relation to the main Sunday services they attended in church.

Comparing frequent churchgoers' experience of Christian youth and community work with our infrequent churchgoers, we conclude that this type of youth work is vital for nurturing the faith of those who are already involved in church, but is less well suited to raising Christian consciousness and stimulating Christian faith amongst those who are not.

Does belief in God or a Christian identity make any difference to how young people live their lives?

Just under half of our infrequent churchgoers believed in some sort of God and identified themselves as Christian. Our last question then, was concerned with what difference this belief and identity makes to these young people's everyday living?

We have already seen that even a vague Christian memory was helpful for shoring up the immanent faith of young people in times of crisis or difficulty. Beyond this, however, we found that our infrequent churchgoers also saw value in Christianity insofar as it potentially provided guidelines for living, although they were not always clear as to what these guidelines actually might be. In an individualized society, our young people found themselves facing many difficult choices and dilemmas about how to live their lives. These were sometimes exacerbated by parents who were either absent, and therefore left young people to get on with their lives on their own; or else were too emotionally involved preferring to befriend and unconditionally support their children in their choices rather than direct them and, in addition, sometimes sharing their own adult problems with their children in return. This friendship parenting forced young people into an early adult role in much the same way that absent parents did. We called this the lost childhood of Generation Y. Our young people therefore welcomed opportunities to explore what makes for a good life and what count as right choices. The youth clubs provided such opportunities and went some way to providing a moral community to which they could relate. Outside of the youth club, however, belief in God *per se* and having a Christian identity hardly informed infrequent churchgoers' decision-making at all. Rather, authenticity was the guiding principle for how to live. In short, young people wanted to be in control of their own decision-making but they also wanted those choices to be informed. Ethics was therefore more of a priority to our infrequent churchgoers than religion.

Somewhat surprisingly perhaps given the various media portrayals of young people, the way our infrequent churchgoers described their approach to living a good life suggested they had a conventional and sensible attitude to life. Their aim was to secure personal happiness for themselves, their family and their friends, they recognized the need to care for others, and they were prepared to work hard at school to get a good job and hopefully eventually to settle down and have a family of their own. They wanted to avoid the mistakes of their parents who had failed marriages, children too young or missed opportunities. Beyond this, our infrequent churchgoers had no over-arching sense of ultimate purpose that might have been associated with a religious outlook. Our young people tended to think in terms of plans rather than purpose and they were content with this.

From our sociological analysis then, it seems that whilst most young people have very little direct engagement with Christianity on a day-to-day basis, the contours of faith in late modernity do still show faint traces of Christian belief and practice. What this means for mission and outreach and the wider Church is taken up Part Two.

PART TWO:
THEOLOGICAL REFLECTION

7

Love is not enough

In this section of the book we are looking to engage in a dialogue between theology and sociology. One of the features of modern theology has been its willingness to engage with the social sciences and to see a real exchange of ideas about the nature of humankind and the realities of contemporary living. The dialogue between sociology and theology has helped the Church to create points of contact between modern-day culture and Christian tradition. Sociology interprets back to the Church what it understands of people's social worlds. It deals with how society views young people and how young people understand their role in the social order. Theology looks at young people's position in front of God. Sociology is good for looking at patterns of contemporary faith but it is the job of theology to interpret what this means for the Church and how to respond to it.

It is at this point in the book we move from Hervieu-Léger (a French sociologist) to Stanley Hauerwas (a Texan theologian). Though sociology and theology are often uncomfortable bedfellows, we have identified common themes in the writing of both these scholars that create a helpful framework for us to analyze the material that we have collected on English Generation Y young people. For Hauerwas, as for Hervieu-Léger, the three components of religion – believing, community and tradition – stand out clearly, though the terminology changes. While Hervieu-Léger refers to 'believing', Hauerwas talks of embodying the Christian story. While a lineage of believers is central to Hervieu-Léger's understanding of religion, for Hauerwas Christianity without the Church community is impossible. Tradition for both Hervieu-Léger and Hauerwas binds it all together, past, present and future. Thus as we move in our discussion from sociology to theology, from religion as a chain of memory to Christianity as storied, traditioned community, we nevertheless retain the continuity of thought between the concepts of the two separate disciplines in understanding young people's faith.

Ecclesiology

The strong emphasis on ecclesiology in the work of Stanley Hauerwas is the antidote to the individualization we have talked about earlier in the book. Hauerwas argues that without the Church, as a community of believers living out the story of God's forgiving love, there is no framework for theological reflection (or ethics). The Church is God's political activity on earth; the congregation is the hermeneutic of the gospel (Newbigin 1989). Religious belief is akin to the performance rather than the text of a play. *King Lear*, for example, needs to be performed for it to be understood; it is the interplay between the actors and the text that makes the play come alive. In church terms it is the point at which the believers engage with the reality of the Scriptures that God's truth comes to life. 'The Scriptures tell the story of the forgiving love of God and the Church is an extended argument over time about the significance of that story and how to interpret it' (Hauerwas 1983:383).

Hauerwas draws a distinction between forgiveness within a family as an act of mutual affirmation and support, and forgiveness in the Church as an act of political liberation. The former is driven by a family narrative which (in our contemporary cultural context) focuses on the emotional needs of its members. A Church narrative that focuses on the possibility of transformation drives the latter. Hauerwas talks of the Church as 'a community capable of forming people with virtues [faith, hope and love (1 Cor. 13)] sufficient to witness to God's truth in the world' (1981b:84). Thomson writes that for Hauerwas 'a tangible and trained character rather than a theoretical belief is the sign of the Church' (2003:9). The ability of Christian discourse to give people a sense of their identity sustains the concrete Church.

Christianity is an incarnated rather than an abstract truth and so it only becomes real when it is embodied in the reality of people's lives. According to Hauerwas' ecclesiology one cannot simply pick up the Bible and read it in order to understand what is meant. This is pertinent to our study since we are seeking to establish the extent to which a knowledge of the faith can be built up through voluntary youth clubs and separately from specifically formed faith communities. The belief that God is Father, Son and Holy Spirit is not a theoretical set of possibilities but one that is acted out within a community of faith; it is this that makes it real. Hauerwas argues that Christians' first political responsibility is to be the Church, and by being the Church they should understand that their first political loyalty is to God.

There are underpinning assumptions to Hauerwas' ecclesiology that echo the work of Michael Polanyi (1891–1976). Polanyi wrote about how knowledge is established within the framework of a wider community of understanding. A scientist in pursuit of knowledge is not an isolated individual unaffected by the rules, directions and discoveries of the wider scientific community. The scientist is under the authority of the scientific community in his pursuit of truth. For the scientist to recognize what is significant or otherwise in the process of discovery, he needs to understand what has already been defined as significant by the scientific community (Polanyi 1983:379). 'The role of science is akin to the role of the Church ... [and] ... the role of the scientist, akin to the role of the theologian' (Polanyi 1983:309).

Hauerwas's ethics and ecclesiology are companions to the work of Alasdair MacIntyre. MacIntyre wrote that there can be no understanding of ethics without a community within which norms and standards of behaviour are established. According to Aristotle (out of which MacIntyre's work is construed) ethical living is decided by one's role as a citizen within the city state. This establishes a shared sense of what makes for a good life and hence also the behaviour appropriate to it. MacIntyre (1985) argues that there is no common understanding of what constitutes a community in our late modern society (our equivalent to the city state). His assertion is that without such an understanding ethics is no longer a matter of priniciples but is actually just a mask for expressions of personal preference.

Hauerwas' thinking offers us a framework not only to interpret what we have learned about the faith of Generation Y but also to consider the role the Church might play with young people in the future. In Hauerwasian terms we could say that Generation Y's learning about the faith has been hindered by a lack of church-type communities to which they feel they can, and want to, belong. As a theological statement of belief the idea of an authentic church community that connects the reality of young people's lives with the story and tradition of the Christian faith is un-contentious. As a social reality it is problematic because the idea of the Church has become freeze framed in many people's minds as an institutional hurdle that needs to be jumped in order to have a personal relationship with Christ. Youth work and Fresh Expressions (www.freshexpressions.org.uk) are the two current Church initiatives intended to bridge this gap. We will look at each of these in turn.

Youth work

We have seen in our study that youth work is only moderately successful in bridging the gap between church and society and in raising young people's Christian consciousness. We are suggesting that the reason for this is that youth workers have tended to adopt a 'strategic liberalism' without this being rooted within an authentic Christian community.

Hauerwas' contention is that the Church has adopted liberalism as a social strategy appropriate to the Christian story (cf Hauerwas 1981a:11). Before we consider this idea it is worth us clarifying what is intended by Hauerwas in using the idea of liberalism in the way that he does. In essence liberalism is the idea that individuals are free to pursue their own goals, in their own ways, provided they do not infringe on the freedom of others. The way in which these principles are interpreted will depend on the context in which they are applied. For example (in a UK context) 'market liberalism' is based on the idea of meritocracy but 'social liberalism' more on equality. 'Market liberalism' means laissez-faire economic policies, a deregulated economy, private ownership and wealth creation as prime political objectives. Social liberalism means civil rights, social justice and an individual right of self-determination. The common theme to both is that the individual is seen as the core unit of society.

In an academic context, liberal theology does not refer to a distinctive set of beliefs, but rather to a way of thinking about Scripture. What is known as the 'historical-critical' approach suggests that the Bible should not be read as eternally valid, verifiable factual statements about God but as documents that outline the human authors' beliefs and feelings about God at the time of its writing (i.e. within their specific historical/cultural context). The liberal theologian would say that while one cannot necessarily speak confidently about God, one could do so about one's experience of God. The liberalism in this is the emphasis given to individual and community interpretations of Scripture.

Hauerwas' peculiarly American liberalism is tied up in the political discourse over the relationship between the Church and state. The separation between the two in the US means that there is an assumption that the churches constantly have to decide how to ally themselves to social and political agendas. This is different from the UK where it is assumed that the role of the Church is to remain impartial. Hauerwas criticizes US conservative Christianity as a political form of 'liberalism' in the way that its presuppositions are shaped by American patriotism. In the introduction to *Against the Nations* (1985) he offers this basic definition of liberalism:

> In the most general terms I understand liberalism to be that impulse deriving from the Enlightenment project to free all people from the chains of their historical particularity in the name of freedom ... [it is an attempt] to free reason from being determined by any particularistic tradition. (Hauerwas 1985:18)

The theme that is pertinent to our research and which we carry back across the Atlantic is the idea that liberalism leads to the loss of the heritage and story of which one is a part. In Hauerwasian terms it is implausible to expect a liberal agenda of personal and social education stripped clean of history and tradition to deliver a theological vision of a new life in Christ. Informal education wants young people to have the right to make their own choices; the Church wants young people to choose what is 'right' and to respond to the historical truth revealed in Christ. These are two different epistemological realities placed alongside each other: the relativism of the former and the objectivism of the latter. A social liberalism where Christianity is seen as a lifestyle choice rather than a revealed truth does little to alleviate this disparity.

The youth workers in our study wanted to treat informal education as a method and keep Christianity as substance. Young people were encouraged to make choices for themselves and the hope was that they would choose Christianity; the overall aim was for them to make informed choices, be this Christianity or not. The difficulty of this position in terms of mission was that the young people were not being informed enough to make a decision either way. For example, there was an implicit assumption among some youth workers in their approach to mission that if they acted in a loving, kind, faithful (i.e. Christian) manner, young people's curiosity would be provoked by their actions and the young people would ask the youth workers about their faith. In not wanting to impose ideas on young people, the youth workers had bought into humanistic 'unconditional positive regard' (Rogers 1980) as a way of working, and were simply playing back to the young people what they already thought of as important (mutual validation in Hervieu-Léger's terms). The young people wanted authenticity; the youth workers reflected this back to them as being important. The logic of liberalism is that any choice is as valid as any other.

The effects of strategic liberalism on how the young people viewed Christianity (when asked directly) are illustrated in a conversation with Sue and Wendy. Sue appeared to accept that the youth workers were Christian and she understood that this was their motivation for what they did. The problem for the Church is that neither she nor Wendy (who talks about karma) appears to care one way or the other. It simply does not matter to them. They are not looking for faith – it's a case of each to their own. The youth club is a leisure-time activity rather than a faith community and there is nothing to suggest to Wendy or Sue that they should see the youth worker's faith as anything more or less significant than any other views they may hold. The conversation went as follows:

Interviewer:	What do you think motivates the youth workers to get involved?
Sue:	God.
Interviewer:	God.
Sue:	Yeah, God.
Interviewer:	That's a very definite answer, can you tell me a bit more about that?
Sue:	Cos they believe and talk about God.
Interviewer:	Do all of them?
Sue:	Not all, but a couple of them and I think they do it cos, well I think that they believe in God and they want God to think that they are doing something good maybe, I don't know . . .
Wendy:	Karma.
Sue:	. . . and they'll go to heaven.
Interviewer:	What do you mean by karma?
Wendy:	You do something good, you get something good back in return.

The answer to Sue and Wendy's indifference to the Christian faith is deceptively simple – an authentic church community that connects the reality of their lives with the story and tradition of the Christian faith. The issue is not the muddle of concepts they hold but the fact that they were not a part of a community that could help them to make sense of what they were thinking. For young people such as Sue and Wendy who either do not realize or else do not care about the youth worker's motivation, love is not enough. They need to know what the love is about if the youth workers' behaviour is going to mean anything more to them than the fact that youth workers are simply nice people.

Corporate truth

The discourse needed for an unstoried generation is one of both story and engagement. The contemporary context needs an approach more akin to the two disciples on the road to Emmaus (Luke 24:15) than to Paul on the road to Damascus (Acts 22:6). Paul was struck by a sudden revelation and had the training and religious background to make sense of what had happened to him. The two disciples, however, needed to work slowly through what had happened in Jerusalem. They knew that the tomb was empty but still chose to leave the city thinking that they had seen all that there was to see. Their realization of what had actually happened came partly through Jesus explaining the Scriptures and partly through him sharing the meal with them. There was an opportunity for both explanation and engagement. Jesus went through the sequence of events while they were walking together and shared with them over the meal. They needed the story retelling to enable them to make sense of the person whom Jesus was when he sat down for the meal, and they needed the meal to make sense of the story they had heard.

There are other parallels and inferences that can be drawn from Scripture. In the early Church the Athenians (Acts 17) were reaching out for God but did not have a language of explanation. They had an inscription in their market place entitled 'To an Unknown God'. Paul told them that what they worshipped as unknown he would make known. The Athenian situation is different from our own because our young people appeared not only to lack the language for God but also, until questioned directly, to lack any particular interest – 'benign indifference' is the phrase that we have been using – it means that young people lack the framework to understand and the inclination to engage.

Generally the young people were not going to progress an understanding of the faith if they did not see themselves as a part of a wider Christian community of discovery. We have talked about 'make do and mend religion'. The young people have a cursory knowledge of the Christian faith and tap into that in times of difficulty; they seem content with what little they know. At best Christianity was seen as a choice made by the youth workers but not one that the young people saw as needing to concern them. The young people were not restlessly seeking God and looking for explanations from the youth workers. They were living out their 'immanent faith', forming their own communities from among family and friends. These family-friends communities were the main potential transmitter of the faith available to the young people. Insofar as these communities lack direct Christian involvement, Christian faith transmission was not happening and so it is unsurprising that an unstoried generation has emerged.

Detach the Christian story from the Christian community and all one is left with are abstract facts and liberal qualities of tolerance, pluralism and respect for personal autonomy. These are then seen to be self-defining and so invalidate the need for story. Hauerwas (1983) repeatedly stresses that freedom and equality are not self-interpreting but require a tradition to give them form. He says that the Church (i.e., the Body of Christ) is devoted not to the principles of memoryless liberalism but, rather, to a story of a particular God and a specific way of life that follows Jesus. The members of the Church know themselves not in the first instance as autonomous and free individuals but as people bound together through a common story and tradition. Hauerwas' contention is that what all the varieties of liberalism have in common is a lack of memory associated with stories.

> Christian freedom can only ever be recovered as the Church recognizes the degree to which it has become emasculated and colonized through its confusion of liberal rhetoric with the narrative of the faith. (Thomson 2003:07)

Fresh Expressions

Ten years of professionalized youth work has been asking the same questions of the Church now being asked by Fresh Expressions among the Methodists, in the United Reformed Church and in the Church of England: what does it mean to be or to do church? How much of a 'church' does a youth club need to be to see a young person engage with the claims of Christ? How does a school exclusion project run on a Tuesday relate to a congregation gathered for worship on a Sunday? Historically youth workers have considered themselves as the poor relations on a church leadership team and so would see themselves as singularly ill equipped to answer this question.

The Fresh Expressions initiative emerged out of the *Mission Shaped Church* report, published in 2004 as the report of a working party set up by the Mission and Public Affairs Council of the Church of England. It aims to create new communities of belonging within which people can learn about the Christian faith. The Report stated that the local parish system is no longer able to meet all the needs of our mobile society and so we should complement it with different types of church gatherings. These other forms of church have become known as 'fresh expressions'.

Youth work, we suggest, suffers from the loss of a conscious Christian narrative due to its willingness to detach itself from traditioned gathered faith communities. The question now is how successful or otherwise the Fresh Expressions initiative is in its attempt to engage people with the Christian faith. The caution in Hauerwas' ecclesiology is that any evangelistic initiative that models itself to people on the grounds of 'we have what you've been looking for' cannot help but be susceptible to the ethics of a market economy. Hauerwas' ecclesiology suggests that without the Christian formation learnt through a church-type gathering, people do not, in eternal terms, actually know 'what they are looking for'. Fresh Expressions – like parish communities – have to cultivate forgiving, learning, discipling relationships in order to reshape people's understanding of reality in the light of God's love.

Fresh Expressions has needed to deal with a church-fatigue from among the Christian constituency. This in turn has trivialized people's expectations of the initiative. Church fatigue shows itself through the assumption that people are drawn towards Jesus but put off by the Church. People like the idea of a 'churchless faith' (Jamieson 2002). Christopher Cocksworth makes reference to a tendency among some of reacting against many of the practices of the Church, preferring to search out the inner reality of spiritual experience rather than the outer layer of religious observance. People underestimate Fresh Expressions when they see it simply as a deconstructed church (there to answer the above) rather than as a gathering with a community-rooted, culturally-attuned ecclesiology in and of itself. Rowan Williams points to the seriousness with which Fresh Expressions addresses the question of Christian truth:

> As Fresh Expressions gets more successful, more widely known, more active and innovative, it's really very important to remember that Fresh Expressions is not first and foremost about capturing a new market for a product ... Fresh Expressions ought to be, and I hope and pray is, part of the Church's way of pushing back against static, infantilising forms of religious belief, pushing back against trivialisation, against the shrinkage of faith and discipleship to boring and manageable dimensions. (Williams 2010)

What we have called 'strategic liberalism' would want us to believe that if the narrative of the faith, the community of believers and the tradition of belief were separated then they can always be put back together again at a later date. However, to detach the Christian narrative from the Christian community jeopardizes the language of faith because without group validation belief can only ever be explained as a personal choice, and the phrase 'Jesus Christ is Lord' will only ever be heard as a matter of opinion. If there is nothing more than 'self' or 'mutual' validation (see Chapter 4) then one loses the durability needed for a language robust enough to talk about God. The Church is left in the position within which it rightly feels uncomfortable, that of trying to persuade people into the faith rather than simply telling (and living out) the story.

Hauerwas (1993) writes that reading the Scriptures 'rightly' is not a given but requires the hard discipline of living as a people constituted by the practices of the risen Lord. Until one has worshipped with, apologized to and lived among a faith community one cannot presume to understand the Scriptures. The memory of the Christian story comes alive through a community of learners, teachers, hearers and doers; all want to understand its significance. When we talk about there being a lack of story among Generation Y we do not simply mean an ignorance over a set of facts about what happened 2000 years ago that could be corrected were one simply to pick up the Scriptures and read them. Being a Christian involves being a part of an on-going tradition of belief; it is not simply a question of assenting to a correct number of propositions, and becoming a Christian is not simply an intuitive human experience where one feels the right thing, in the right time, in the right place and makes a commitment in faith. To suppose that we can hold Christianity at arm's length and decide upon its merits from a perspective entirely independent of it is an epistemological error.

Hauerwas talks of the Church as a community of character, storied, embodied and in ongoing formation (1981a). When Jesus challenged the rich young ruler to sell all he had and give to the poor he did not ask him what he felt and to reflect on what he had heard. He invited him to join with the disciples who were together working through what it meant to follow Jesus (Mark 10:21).

Young people and Fresh Expressions

According to its own publicity, young people are not the primary focus of Fresh Expressions. The initiative works primarily with adults: 9 in 10 (89%), in fact, involve adults over 25 years of age. A large number, over 2 in 3 (69%), involve children less than 16 years of age while 1 in 3 (33%) involves young people aged between 16 and 25 years (Church of England 2007). Dave Male says this of the situation:

> Those with no previous or present church experience ... [are] ... a group that is continually growing and include the youngest sector of society ... [and] ... is the group that according to any statistics we are struggling to make contact with (Male 2008:153, 151).

Fresh Expressions and young people are bound together by a desire for authenticity. Fresh Expressions suggest that people are looking for authentic spirituality. Our research suggests that young people are looking for authentic lifestyles. They want to know what difference contact with the Church would make to how they live and not simply to what they feel. The relative lack of contact with young people leaves us asking about how far the ethos of Fresh Expressions fits with the rationale of Generation Y that we have identified through the research.

The intellectual roots of Fresh Expressions lie in the missionary writings of Roland Allen (1985), Vincent O Donovan (1982), Lesslie Newbigin (1989) and John V Taylor (1972). Allen was an early advocate of establishing churches, which from the beginning would be self-propagating, self-governing and self-financing. In the spirit of St Paul, the missionary should lay down principles and leave the local church to work through the implications. Donovan applied these principles to his work with the Masai tribe in Africa and Newbigin brought it back to the UK following his time abroad in India. The ethos for Fresh Expressions has been fired by John Taylor's (1972) comment that we should find out what God is doing in the world and join in; and also by Donovan's much quoted comment that:

> The missionary's job is to preach, not the Church, but Christ. If he preaches Christ and the message of Christianity, the Church may well appear, but it might not be the Church he had in mind. (Donovan 1982:81)

The implication from the period following Donovan's work in Africa is that there will be a second phase of the Fresh Expressions initiative that will absorb lessons from its elder sister – the inherited expressions of church (Gamble 2006). After Donovan the African churches moved away from pure indigenization wanting to draw on the wider knowledge and expertise of the Western Church. As a result there exists today the paradox of Western missionaries encouraging enculturation and an African hierarchy rejecting it. The first phase of Fresh Expressions has paralleled Donovan working to create self-determining groups of believers, which can develop under their own constructs free from any centralizing bureaucratic influence.

If the African process is followed through we will swing back towards integrated models of church, and this renewed traditionalism will fit comfortably with the inter-generational ethos of Generation Y young people. The Church appears to want the young people to discover their own way of being church. The young people do not want to be left to their own devices. They live in an adult world and are used to integrating different parts of their lives. They are comfortable with cross-generational relationships. They will not be swamped by traditional as the Church fears they might.

A Generation X worldview read back into the emerging Generation Y?

The elder end of Generation X, now in positions of church leadership, were likely to have been brought up by wartime parents. This meant a tight parenting structure with a need to step away from the family in order to create their own social spaces. When they became parents they were determined to ensure that there was not the same distance between them and their children. In Chapters 3 and 5 we look at how they made friends with their children and created a generation encouraged to work hard, achieve good grades and a job, conventional in outlook and able to see the value of social rules. Young people do not need to rebel against their parents because generally they can achieve what they want without having to do so. They do not need to change the culture drastically to have their own spaces; rather they could have their own private place, right in the middle of the rest of the family home. Bedrooms are their areas of control, where they project manage their lives.

This suggests that it is wrong to assume that young people will have an inbuilt hostility towards the Church in a way that someone older might. Smith and Denton (2005) make the same point through their research into young people's spiritualities in the USA. They echo the idea that those currently in church leadership are reading their own world view back into the emerging generation:

> Some middle aged religious leaders may project their own experience of the 1960s and 1970s onto teenagers today, but that is a mistake ... the assumption that teenagers are alienated from their parents and hostile toward religion is a deep-rooted but flawed stereotype. Any generation gap that exists between teens and adults today is superficial compared with and far outweighed by generational continuities. (Smith with Denton 2005:266, 264)

We have explored earlier the way in which young people are mapping out their own choices but are following conventional routes in so doing. Young people are used to a high level of adult interaction and so will not be automatically put off by multigenerational church worship. The family is the ultimate point of reference and this is reflected in how they relate to those around them. Their moral thinking is developed within their families and through relationships with those older than themselves. There is a moral seriousness to how they relate to the world and this is best met by a corresponding seriousness in the Church with the development of character and morality high on its agenda. The indication is that they would be no less willing to engage with authentic (and non-dull) traditional forms of worship than they would be with a fresh expression of a church.

Alongside family closeness and social conservatism, there are many young people who do not know enough about the Church to be put off it. Some young people will have close interfamilial relationships and will be involved in the Church because of parents or siblings. However it cannot automatically be assumed that a Generation Y young person will be more attracted to a 'fresh' than to a 'traditional' expression of church. They will, at the least, be no more hostile to a traditional than to a fresh expression because they do not have the history of involvement to be so. A fresh expression has more appeal to those who are bored or unfulfilled by traditional church (Wilkinson 2008).

The strength of Fresh Expressions is its desire to create new communities of belief. When these communities are able to absorb the historical narrative of the faith then they are touching the heart of what is required for the Church to connect with young people in a meaningful manner – 'the Church is most relevant to society when it is self-regarding' – 'The purpose of the Church is not to make the world a better place but to bear witness to Christ and to help the world to understand the true nature of reality' (Hauerwas 1981b:47).

What now?

If contextualizing theology in the name of youth and community work, or encouraging Fresh Expressions of church, does not appear to have connected with an unstoried Generation Y then we need to dig further in order to understand why this might be so. Lining up the usual suspects (family, church, school, peers, etc.) will not help us. The underlying issues go deeper than this. Improving our communication skills or being more sophisticated in our service delivery may help but they do not answer the fundamental epistemological question that lies beneath the failure of the Church to connect with an un-storied Generation Y.

What are the underlying issues? One is the subjectivization of belief and the other is the adoption of social liberalism as a functional truth. Both of these two squeeze out the need for a distinctive Christian narrative. The former is self-referential and ignores the traditioned, community-embodied nature of the Christian story. This creates a self-perpetuating subjectivization. It reduces faith to an emotion rather than to an engagement with a community of belief. The latter is self-validating and squeezes out the particularity of the Christian story. Liberal values such as tolerance and diversity, personal autonomy and individual choice are memory-less. They have no need of story. Without the story they have no narrative of well-being and without this there is no reason for anyone to look beyond their immediate empirical reality.

Remember well

In 'Love's not all you need' Hauerwas (1981b) notes that the gospel is not about abstract notions of love, but about the story of Jesus Christ. The fundamental category of human flourishing is not freedom but knowing the narrative of which one is a part. In Scripture the Israelites learn the character of God by remembering the stories of what he has done. They are told to remember that they were slaves in Egypt and that the Lord God redeemed them (Deuteronomy 15:15).

The Psalmists draw the connection between community formation and the chain of cultural-religious memory. For the Israelites a loss of cultural memory meant a loss of story and a loss of story meant a loss of social identity (cf Brueggemann 1986). The Psalmist asks the Israelites, exiled in Babylon, what the significance was of their previous life in Jerusalem? How did their memories of Jerusalem shape the understanding they had of themselves and what role did these memories play in their new life in Babylon?

> By the rivers of Babylon we sat and wept when we remembered Zion . . . How can we sing the songs of the Lord while in a foreign land? (Psalm 137:1, 4)

If the Israelites did not learn how to 'sing the Lord's song' they would have become absorbed into the Babylonian culture because there would no longer have been anything distinctive in who they were. It is their history, story and community that make them who they are. Remembering their past is key to retaining their identity as the people of God. 'If I forget you, O Jerusalem', continues the Psalmist,

> may my right hand forget its skill, may my tongue cling to the roof of my mouth if I do not remember you, if I do not consider Jerusalem my highest joy. (Psalm 137:5-6)

Brueggemann writes that 'Psalm 137 is a passionate resolve not to be assimilated . . . [it is a] polemical theological imagination that guards against cultural assimilation' (1986:103, 110).

The primary challenge that Generation Y makes to the Church is to maintain its collective identity as the people of faith living out the stories of God. Society refers happily to Christian values but not to the Christian story that makes sense of those values. When the story is lost the community is no longer grounded in tradition. What makes the Church distinctive is stories and metaphors rather than habits and rules of behaviour.

When Christian principles are challenged publicly, the Church does not know how to respond if it has lost the habit of being guided by story rather than by abstract principles. Deprived of the historical community narrative of which they are a part Christians become simply another interest group and are being treated as such by society. If the Church loses the exegetical skill of understanding social reality and practice from the perspective of Scripture, when liberalism turns round and bites, the Church can do no more than insist on its right to be heard, thus appealing to the same value base that has put it in that position in the first place. The starkness of the issue at hand is shown by the flash points in society reported in the national press during 2009 when religion and secular values came into conflict. Caroline Petrie was suspended as a community nurse after asking an elderly woman patient during a home visit if she wanted her to say a prayer for her (BBC News 2009). Miss Eweida was suspended as an air stewardess for wearing a cross (BBC News 2006). Jennie Cain was suspended as a school receptionist after e-mailing her friends asking for their prayers when her daughter was told off for talking about God and heaven during a lesson at the school (Gammell 2009).

Hauerwas argues for a counter-cultural, distinctive and separate community of belief to shape out the reality of God's love in the world. He directly addresses the reality of church decline and marginalization within society. His writing is a plea to the Church to rediscover its identity as the people of God and to recover its nerve to engage directly with society. His ecclesiology offers a way of articulating the Church–world relationship and expressing the social and political implications of Christianity. When Jesus told the crowd to 'repent and believe because the Kingdom of God was at hand' (Mark 1:15), he was inviting people to engage with a new transcendent reality made possible by his coming to earth.

The danger for a church that focuses too strongly on 'practical apologetics' and on being 'relevant' is that when it over identifies with society it loses its distinctiveness and hence its ability to transform people's lives. A basic lack of working knowledge about the faith means that young people do not have a dualistic worldview in the sense of connecting immediate events with an underpinning Christian narrative. To a Generation Y young person bread and wine are simply bread and wine and not sacramental symbols. In one instance in our study the cross was seen as a club logo and not the central symbol of the Christian faith.

When the Church can no longer rely on being understood, even to the extent of enabling people to disagree with its message, it trips itself up when it tries too hard to identify with the surrounding culture. With people who do not know the rudimentary details of the Christian faith, the Church can be so keen to contextualize that it loses the ability to transform. The desire to be relevant to the surrounding culture can trump the need to be faithful to the Christian story.

In summary, if the Church does not concern itself with mystery, transcendence and worship then it might as well pack up and go home (Martin 2002:140). In Hauerwas' thinking the gospel is not a welfare agenda or the blueprint for an ideal society but rather the proclamation that the Kingdom is among us (Thomson 2003:10).

8

A life of faith

Our dialogue between sociology and theology reaches its natural conclusion in apologetics, the theological discipline that concerns itself with how the gospel should be presented mindful of the particular culture and context in which this is to happen. Every generation of apologists has needed to handle different kinds of questions and issues. Missiologist David Bosch (1991) has said that the mission of the Church needs constantly to be renewed and reconceived. 'The fatal pedagogical error', wrote Tillich (1951), 'is to throw answers like stones at the heads of those who have not yet asked the questions'. Generation Y young people have different concerns and points of interest to those held by the current generation of church leaders. Once these are understood the Church can address itself to the questions being asked of it. Apologetics assumes some common ground between the Christian message and the contemporary society in which it is exercised.

The strongest impression left with us from our research is that of a generation of people without a cohesive Christian story to underpin their place in the world. What is salutary for the Church is that generally young people seemed quite content with this, happy to get by with what little they knew about the Christian faith and willing to draw strength from the Church in times of difficulty or crisis. This leaves a dwindling Church as the holder of the Christian memory retelling and living out the story of God's redemption through its corporate life together.

We have identified a serious minded generation. In 'A good life' (Chapter 5) we talked about young people who have grown up more quickly than their parents' generation; they are well practised at engaging with adult issues. We argued that this has left them willing to deal with lifestyle choices at an early age – the question that they are asking is not so much 'how do I feel about something?' but 'what do I do about it?' In 'Bedroom spirituality' (Chapter 3) we saw how the central place for their thinking, reflection and life management lies at the heart of the family home in the bedroom. Young people are emotionally adept and socially capable because they are used to operating beyond their comfort zone. Internet issues and adult company have left them used to integrating different parts of their lives.

Set against this we can see how the Church's presentation of the gospel has been shaped by the views of the previous Generation X. They have translated their teenage right to an 'adolescent rebellion' into the assumption that young people will want to take the same approach and distance themselves from the Church in order then to decide how to respond. The current generation of church leaders are haunted by the disjuncture between the Christian claims of the gospel and the reality of the Church in society, and are driven by the desire to make one relevant to the other. They have grown up with a strong narrative of the faith and the declining influence of the Church and they have struggled to bring the two together.

The irony is that, without always realizing it, they have achieved a lot of what they set out to do. The Church has ensured its relevance to young people, not least through the resources it has put into Christian youth and community work. There is a double irony in that not only have church leaders underestimated what they have achieved but the young people have also not recognized this provision for what it is and so there has been little connection made in their minds between the Christian faith and how they want to live. Youth workers provided the young people with examples of how to live out the reality of the Christian faith but the young people did not understand that this was what they were trying to do. Youth work has proved itself adept in building relationships but less able to provide young people with an understanding of the Christian narrative. Hence our conclusion that youth work has been more successful in building on what people already know about the faith than in teaching it from scratch.

Generation Y have fewer cultural hang-ups about the Church than did their predecessors. They are 'unstoried' and so do not have the same religious-social framework to reconcile. The challenge to the Church is to provide them with the opportunities to explore and to learn about a narrative of belief of which they know little. There is no reason, from a Generation Y perspective, why this should not happen. Young people are schooled into making connections between different parts of their life and drawing on cultural resources they might feel to be helpful. Liberation for them will not come through freedom from adult interference while they make these lifestyle choices but through an awareness of the Christian narrative which shapes the world of which they are a part.

We have suggested that there has been a shift in cultural consciousness over the way that Christianity and the Church are perceived. The young people in our study were willing to be involved in an adult world; they did not shy away from authority and they did not necessarily want to be left alone in separate peer groups. They were willing to turn to the Church in times of difficulty or crisis and draw strength from its tradition, community and belief. None of this means that young people will come flocking back to church, but they are willing, on occasion, to reflect on and to engage with an issue when it directly affects them. In our research this happened most often over ethics and lifestyle choices.

The young people enjoyed issue-based conversations. Colin talked about how the youth group had helped him through discussion groups, to think about what's important in life. These included issues like 'cruelty, slavery, hunger and poverty'. The young people liked the fact that the youth workers gave them advice but would leave the final decision to them. Rachel said that the youth group helped her with decisions, but it came back to the individual in that helpful discussions are 'just opinions and having a good chat and reflecting [on] things'. They were happy to talk about issues of 'right' and 'wrong'.

This makes the question of lifestyle the key issue for Christian apologetics and a clear potential point of transition into belief. The young people were not interested in faith as a propositional truth but they wanted to know what difference it would make to their lives. For the young people the key question was not 'Is it true?' but 'Does it work?' They want to know what a life of faith might look like in practice. Rowan Williams (2008:4) uses the writing of Dostoevsky to suggest that there is a cultural amnesia as to what this might be. Dostoevsky, he writes, presents a picture of what faith and the lack of it would look like in the political and social world of his day.

Community

The Christian vision for humanity is for a Church where all people relate to each other in the name of Christ (Galatians 3.28) and live out the story of God's forgiving love from one generation to the next. This theological truth became a template for how we interpreted the young people's faith. The youth work tended to provide temporary and transitional communities but not deliberate 'church' type gatherings where young people could learn about the faith. In our research a Christian consciousness only began to take root when the young people were able to engage with and to feel a part of a community of people trying together to live out the gospel story. We saw that the youth work was effective at nurturing frequent churchgoers' Christian faith.

In our research the Church still had a specific role to play for young people at particular moments of need. The young people expressed an interest in death and a willingness to look to the Church for direction. They wanted the Church to exercise its traditional role of providing a ritual for death. There has been a change in attitudes towards social mourning since the death of Princess Diana in 1997. Memorial websites are big business – www.gonetoosoon.co.uk sets up 3000 each year. Church leaders who feel themselves to be marginalized at funerals when worshippers prefer contemporary songs to traditional hymns need not worry. Young people still look to the Church to provide them with a narrative of death. Church leaders are still expected to be on hand when people feel the need for a bit of ceremony in their lives – for Christmas, for weddings and, of course, for funerals (Barley 2006:16, 24).

In the absence of a church membership young people participate in their own communities of belonging and there is a role for the Church in nurturing and working with each of these different people-groupings. Youth work has had particular success in creating self-validating communities, which can in themselves go part way towards creating a community of faith. Memory-making is a skill of the youth worker and can help to build up a sense of tradition and community. This means creating opportunities for young people to experience something which will provide them with a positive memory and which gives an opportunity to revisit the experience. Shared experiences create a living tradition of time spent together and shape the culture for a group of people. Jason talks of a sense of psychological community which involves developing 'traditions, norms, and values that are tied to the settings or communities in which we live' (1997:75), which can involve those working with young people telling their stories in ways that clearly connect to the tradition of which they are a part.

Memory-making tied to social action had a particular resonance for young people looking for authenticity and engagement. A small urban church in Birmingham joined in the Soul Survivor project Slum Survivor and built a slum in front of the church and the young people slept out in it in solidarity with young people in South Africa who live like this all the time. It is now part of the story of the youth group at that church. People say 'Remember when . . .' and the shared experience evokes memories of teamwork, of consciousness raising, of their picture in the local paper and the achievement of camping out in a shelter they had built themselves.

Family

The most significant community of which the young people are a part is their family. Our research has established that the (extended) family is as, or in some instances more, important than friends to Generation Y. The Church is uniquely placed to reflect this in its work and to build up communities of belonging across different generations. Child protection issues notwithstanding, a primary resource that the Church can offer to young people is the opportunity for them to build nurturing and supportive relationships with adults.

Most recently youth work has been echoing some of the intergenerational nature of family living. In July 2008 the National Youth Agency launched a series of pilot studies focusing on skill share, health, heritage and legacy and the arts. Jason Gardner has explored this issue from a Christian perspective in a book called *Mend the Gap*. He observes that the mission statement of the Church is to unite people across divisions but that this is in contrast to our consumer based society, which encourages social groupings around peers and interests. Gardner wants churches to reconnect generations, creating positive rites of passage for the transition between childhood and adulthood; making relationships core across the whole Church so that young people grow up in a context where people can learn from the life stories of others.

Character

We have identified an individualized approach to a life of faith through what we have called 'bedroom spirituality'. James (2001) found that young people used the bedroom to hide public displays of emotion particularly when they were upset and needed to cry or express anger. Just as the youth worker's memory making can be part way towards a community of faith so also can bedroom spirituality be part way towards a life of faith. The young people praying in their bedrooms was an activity largely disengaged from a corporate practice of the faith. There was a 'monastic' type spirituality of withdrawal from a world of multiple choices to a place where they could feel in control.

We termed one aspect of young people's bedroom prayers as 'confession'. Interplay between private and public practice could help to create a conscious connection between 'confession' and 'forgiveness'. Forgiveness is integral to a life of faith in that it underpins all other ways of looking at the world. One of the positive elements of confession is the capacity to experience forgiveness. Pargament and Rye (1998) suggest that experiencing forgiveness gives young people the possibility of encountering two types of peace, peace of mind through healing emotional wounds and peace with others through helping them deal with incidents that have caused them difficulties. They go on to argue that 'although the individual may have removed himself or herself from organized religion, forgiveness may have developed a "religious functional autonomy" of its own; it retains sacred value even though the individual has separated from the institutions and beliefs that gave birth to the value' (1998:68–9).

Location

It would be easy to assume that with an internet-resourced, social-networked, mobile-phoned generation, place, in the sense of a geographical location, would not be that important – what difference does it make if one is sending a text from a friend's house or on a street corner? Facebook provides the social engagement and so why should it matter where one might log on to the Internet? *Mission Shaped Church* (2004:2) argues that we are a network society where the importance of place is secondary to the importance of flows of information, and surely this is the case?

Contrarily we found that this was not necessarily so. The internet did not negate the importance of location; it brought information and social management under the young people's control and into their personal space. Virtual space and physical location blend together – it is not one or the other but both. When a young person was killed in a knife incident, his friends set up an online memorial site but they also put flowers where the event occurred. They wanted to gather together in a church to pray and to light candles.

> Churches are often the only bodies within a community that provide public and open places for tears, grief and remembrance. (Percy 2006:13)

The spiritual expression of worship needs an emotional connection with a physical location. Internet sophistication and territorial affiliation run together.

> Places provide the geography for our imagination; identity is formed, nurtured and fostered by place. (Inge 2003:130)

We identified the importance of place in our earlier work on young people's world view and popular culture (Savage et al. 2006). We found that the young people's pattern of listening to music was location-specific. When they heard a piece of music they could remember where they were when they listened to it previously. Bennett (2000) uses the idea of 'locality' to indicate that young people's music and listening choices are always connected with specific places and contexts. In this instance music simply mirrored the young people's self-perception back to them.

The idea of reflecting back to young people what they already consider to be important is a recurring theme throughout the book. We have identified that youth work has been more able to nurture than to create an interest in the Christian faith and hence played a limited role in translating the faith beyond a natural or otherwise inquiring constituency. We have recognized that the modern family tends to shape itself round the emotional needs of its members and hence is ill equipped to pass on a tradition of Christian thought and belief. Our interest in the significance of geography is that when places are connected in the young people's minds with a public religious narrative it breaks the process of simply mirroring back to young people what they already consider to be important.

Sacralized youth work

A sense of the spiritual importance of place has never been lost within the Church with an unbroken tradition of pilgrimage: trips to the Holy Land, the rediscovery of Iona by the Church of Scotland or Lindisfarne or Walsingham by Anglicans. There are reckoned to be 6000 shrines and sites in Western Europe, now drawing as many as 100 million pilgrims annually. Philip Jenkins (2007) says that the continuing popularity of pilgrimages undercuts any suggestion that European Christianity is dead; he suggests that the pilgrimage may reinvent and reinvigorate European Christianity.

There is a role for youth workers and others in using physical signs and symbols as markers to engender a sense of holiness. We refer to this as 'sacralized youth work' (Nash 2009). Sacralized youth work links an individualized and subjective shaping of belief with identified physical places. It seeks to provide a lens through which those working with young people can be aware of the need to connect the relationships they form with the places they occupy and the faith tradition they are from. 'Land is never simply physical dirt, but is always freighted with social meanings derived from historical experience' (Brueggemann 2002:3).

Sacralized youth work provides places for young people to take part in ritual with sacred connotations, and/or to interact with symbols with a sacred meaning. It is undertaken by those working with young people who have both intention and awareness as to how they might bring a sense of the sacred into the environments in which they work. In our research we identified activities undertaken by the youth workers that could be considered as such. We saw youth workers building a sense of place (residentials), connecting young people to the Christian story (videos, Christian courses, story telling), to ritual with sacred connotations (such as the labyrinth or prayer) and to symbols with sacred meaning (such as religious symbols or imagery around the building).

Our interest is in where young people were able to connect places with, not simply their own story, but also a public religious narrative: church buildings were one example. There was evidence of a Christian consciousness being developed through the physical dimension itself – buildings and locality. Harvey believes that 'the social preservation of religion as a major institution within this secular society has been in part won through the successful creation, protection and nurturing of symbolic places' (1993:23).

Virtual reality offers free-floating intimacies which promise but do not deliver the sense of belonging for which people crave. The young people still wanted to feel connected to physical places. A 'mission shaped geography' can create places that enable people to have a shared and meaningful history together. Simone Weil wrote that 'to be rooted is perhaps the most important need of the human soul' (1952:41).

Ethics and authenticity

In our research we identified two gaps in young people's understanding of ethics. The first was a gap between knowledge and example. Youth workers could provide an example of what a life of faith might look like due to their own and the organization's faith motivation but the young people did not always make a connection between faith and action. Young people's idealism and concern for the future expressed itself through micro-ethics (day-to-day living) as well as through macro-causes (the environment, poverty in the developing world, etc.). We have already identified that lifestyle questions are of interest to young people and can offer transition points into the Christian faith (cf Drane 2008:89).

The second gap was between knowledge and practice. We have seen how young people dealt with sophisticated ethical issues but often lacked the moral grounding to know how to cope and were left feeling out of their depth. Friendship parenting leaves a gap in offering emotional affirmation and support over and above training in a tradition of thought and belonging. 'Parents are more concerned that the children are able to make intelligent choices than that they should know the heritage of which they are a part' (Hauerwas 1983:169). A study released by the Scout Association in the United Kingdom in January 2007 echoes this idea that young people have been left with a self-validating code of ethics. It concludes that young people have to trust their intuition and instincts to decide right from wrong (nfpSynergy 2007:4). They also regard family members as the most positive influences in their lives, have strong beliefs and a desire to make the world a better place (but also want to have fun) (nfpSynergy 2007:27).

Those working with young people accompany them through this journey towards authenticity. The image of 'Odyssey guides' has emerged as a metaphor through our reflections and discussions. An odyssey is a long series of wanderings or adventures filled with notable experiences. Young people often want to be accompanied in this transition time of their lives and those working with young people using their informal education skills can reflect back, guide, lead, encourage, provide opportunities, bring fresh insights, respect and value young people in such a way that they begin to see and have the confidence to follow new paths that may be emerging from the mist of the future.

Authentic Church

We can devise a theological framework to understand the faith world of Generation Y by mapping the lives that young people lead onto markers of the Christian belief. Youth clubs, family and friendship groups offer glimpses of a church community of faith. Praying in their bedroom offers glimpses of a Christian heritage to their spirituality. Church buildings can offer a glimpse of Christian tradition. A concern for the ethical wellbeing of themselves and others offers a glimpse of Christian truth. There were other points of overlap.

We found young people willing to engage with issues of ethics and morality. A result of friendship parenting is that they tend to build on (rather than react against) their parents' values. They do their ethical thinking on their parents' shoulders and want to know what things mean in practice. Ethical lifestyle choices appeared to offer a transition point into discussions about the faith.

We found that, while not necessarily involved with the Church, the young people appreciated its role in society. This was particularly so at points of difficulty and need when young people would look to the Church to provide them with a point of reference. They wanted the Church to provide them with a narrative for death.

We found that church buildings made an impression on young people when they ventured into them. The places where they spent their time became a significant part of their social identity.

We noted the central importance of the family and the willingness of young people to build relationships with adults.

There is logic in all of these examples that the Church would be best spending its time on its natural strengths – ethics and morality, tradition and buildings, family and community are the meat and drink of church life. Hence our conclusion, at the end of four years of endless late nights and long conversations, is that while the primary theological responsibility for the Church is to give glory to God, the primary social responsibility for the Church is simply to be its own authentic self.

THEOLOGICAL EPILOGUE

9

Authentic Church

The authentic self of the Church

A few months ago Bob Mayo approached me to write a concluding response to this research project. He told me that he thought its findings were likely to chime with some of the themes that we mused over during our time together as colleagues at Ridley Hall and the Centre for Youth Ministry in Cambridge; themes which I have explored more fully in my book *Holding Together: Gospel, Church and Spirit* (Cocksworth 2008). I knew from my days of working with Bob that when he has a hunch about something it is worth stopping and listening. He has a habit of seeing what is coming and being a few steps ahead of the rest of us.

I am glad that I followed my instinct of following Bob's instinct, because this piece of research, together with its sociological and theological reflections (neither of which I had any part in), go right to the heart of what I was trying to say in *Holding Together*. The conviction with which I had arrived as an evangelical Christian, and which I tried to expand in the book, is that there is *no gospel without the Church*, just as, of course, there is *no Church without the gospel*. Over a number of years I came to see that I had been so keen to stress the immediacy of our relationship with Christ that I had downplayed the mediation of his presence and activity through his Body. It is also important to recognize that there is *no gospel without the Spirit*, for Christ and his gospel come to us by the Spirit; and that there is *no Church without the Spirit*, for the Spirit activates and animates the Church. In the language of the massive challenge with which the last chapter of this present book ended, I came to realize that the authentic self of Christianity is found in the holding together of these great themes of gospel, Church and Spirit. Hence, the Church is most authentically itself when it rises to the measure of its full stature in Christ (Ephesians 4.13), by receiving, celebrating and sharing Christ's gospel in his Spirit.

I called this shape of Christian life a *catholic form of evangelicalism in the Spirit*. Names are not important though, and others may prefer a different configuration of those words. What is important is the simple truth that the Church is that community in which, through the working of the Spirit, the gospel is seen and heard. The good news of new life is passed on by Christ's followers to those who have become or are becoming followers of Israel's Messiah in a movement of witness that stretches back to the first apostles, as the opening of 1 John makes clear.

> We declare to you what was from the beginning, what we have heard, what we have seen with our eyes, what we have looked at and touched with our hands, concerning the word of life – this life was revealed, and we have seen it and testify to it, and declare to you the eternal life that was with the Father and was revealed to us – we declare to you what we have seen and heard so that you also may have fellowship with us; and truly our fellowship is with the Father and with his Son Jesus Christ (1 John 11–3).

It is worth thinking about this New Testament pattern of passing on because it takes us to one of the key words and themes that emerged from this research. Paul reminds the Church of Corinth that he 'handed on to [them] as of first importance what [he] had in turn received: that Christ died for our sins in accordance with the Scriptures, and that he was buried, and that he was raised on the third day in accordance with the Scriptures, and that he appeared to Cephas, then to the twelve' (1 Corinthians 15.3–5). Paul is a point in a process of transmission. He received the news of Christ's death and resurrection and then handed over that news to the Corinthians. The Greek verb that Paul uses to describe his passing on of the news is *paradidomi* from the same cluster of words as the noun *paradosis*, meaning tradition. Paul had 'traditioned' the gospel to the Corinthians – he had handed on the *paradosis*, the tradition, which had been placed in his hands.

In handing over the news about Jesus' death and resurrection, Paul is handing over more than a message about Christ (he is 'traditioning' more than information). He is communicating the *content* of the news, that which makes it really good news – Jesus Christ himself. When people truly receive this tradition (this *paradosis* which is being handed to them) they are receiving Christ himself:

> *As you therefore have received Christ Jesus the Lord*, continue to live your lives in him, rooted and built up in him and established in the faith, just as you were taught, abounding in thanksgiving (Colossians 2.6, emphasis added).

Paul's teaching on the Lord's Supper illustrates this pattern even more fully. He 'received from the Lord what [he] handed on' to the Corinthians (1 Corinthians

11.23). The tradition orginates with the Lord. It is received by the Apostles. It is passed on by them to those who receive it and then handed on by them to others who are ready to receive it, and who then keep up the pattern of transmission (the *traditioning* of the *tradition*). Note, though, that what is handed on is not just information about the Last Supper foretelling the death of Christ. It is a *practice* that celebrates his victory over death and that enjoys the presence of his risen life in the Christian community as it awaits the fullness of his coming on the last day. It is the *Lord's* Supper. Jesus' body and blood – the reality of his life given over for death but now risen and active – is given to his people to be received by his people. The presence of his risen life is available to his body as we gather around him as he comes to us, we listen to his word burning hope deep within us, we draw near to his table as he makes himself known to us in the breaking of the bread, and then we go and tell others that he is risen indeed (Luke 24.13–35).

All of this is there in 1 John quoted a moment ago. What they *saw and heard* with their own eyes (1) was Jesus himself; and it is Jesus whom they are declaring to us through the Spirit in the *practice of reading and hearing Scripture* so that we may have fellowship with them, with Christ and the with the Father (3). They are not just telling us words concerning life, they are communicating the Word of life (1): the life that was revealed to them and to which they now testify through words of Scripture (4).

The research into the faith of Generation Y has shown that this generation, despite (perhaps because of) its distance from the Church is not particularly hostile towards Christian faith. Indeed, the memory of Christianity is still sufficiently audible for young people to turn to the Church at critical moments in life for support. Moreover, many are open to hearing from the Church and its faith as they seek to shape their identity and navigate through the moral complexities of life. The challenge to the Church is to be confident in the one it is commending and in the fundamental practices by which it makes him known.

The rest of this chapter will reflect on how what we have to say 'concerning the word of life' relates to some of the characteristics of selfhood and identity for young people that the research reveals. It will then go on to explore how the message of the Faith cannot be dissociated from the medium of the Church and its practices. The apostle Peter will figure as an ancient example of what remains true today.

The gospel and the authentic self of Generation Y

The research describes the faith of Generation Y as immanent and this-worldly. It is a faith that members of the generation have in their families, their friends and themselves as they seek to shape their identities authentically in relation to those around them and to their own aspirations. What does the gospel of Jesus Christ have to say to this immanent faith and its various components? In what way is it good news to the Generation Y pictured in this research?

The gospel attends to the limited and flawed character of human existence. To the self that seeks to shape its life by reference to this world and its capacities, it offers the prospect of being re-shaped by the transcending categories of the kingdom of God and empowering capacities of Jesus Christ. For Generation Y relationships are the key to a happy life. This is a profound insight about the nature and purpose of human life. It is one of the many values of this generation that rightly give us hope that 'our future ... is in good hands'.[1] At the same time, defined only within the self-limited and flawed boundaries of human life, it is self-defeating. As Generation Y knows better than most, human relationships – even those we should be able to rely on most securely – are inherently unstable. Relationships require trust and people are not always trustworthy. Indeed, we know that we are not always trustworthy in our relationships with others just as we know well that others cannot always be relied upon. What do we do with our own fallibility and with the fallibility of those to whom we entrust ourselves? Is there a father and family, a brother and friend who can be fully relied upon and can provide the environment in which our own failings can be forgiven and the failing of others towards us be healed?

In Christian terms there is – and it is found in the fellowship that Christ has with his Father into which the Spirit welcomes us. This most transcendent of relationships – the communion of the divine life – is extended into the immanence of human life to affirm the wholesome human drive for relationship and community (for friends and family) and to transcend all that we can ask or imagine (Ephesians 3.20).

This pattern of divine relationships into which we are drawn through Jesus Christ extends, through the humanity of Christ, into a pattern of human relationships. Indeed, by being in communion with Christ, we are in communion with all those with whom he has communion. His own mother is our mother (John 19.27). Those who cry out *Abba! Father!* in his Spirit are our brothers and sisters (Galatians 4.6–7). Those for whom he prays and is calling to follow him are those we are seeking to reach in his name (Matthew 28.19–20). Our network of relationships goes further, for Christ is the one in whom all things were made and in whom all things hold together (Colossians 1.15–17). We are bound to the whole creation through him, yearning that all things will be set free from their present decay (Romans 8.18–21). We are not baptized into a private relationship with Christ, even though it is an intensely personal one. We are baptized into 'one body' (1 Corinthians 12.13), one 'large family' (Romans 8.29) that extends beyond the intensity of our immediate contacts through layers and levels of extensity into one vast network, the reality of which perhaps only present generations have the experience to grasp through the international, non-proximate networks made possible by today's technology.

The deep-seated human need to belong, together with the basic human instinct to care for those to whom we belong, lies at the heart of Christian faith. It is the story of Scripture, beginning with Adam and fulfilled in the New Jerusalem. It is the basis of Christian ethics. The network of relationships into which we are created, the family into which we are redeemed and the kingdom to which we are moving, carry responsibilities. Generation Y, conscious more than any other generation of the interdependence of life, want to live responsibly. They want to find ways of expressing the freedom and integrity of the self that do not restrict or impede the free space of 'the other'. But that is easier said than done. Perspectives are needed which see beyond the limited vision of one's own self and one's family and friends. Furthermore, empowerment is needed to curtail the freedom of oneself in order to give space for the freedom of the other and, in so doing, to find one's fullest integrity.

The Christian story speaks about the dignity of human beings made in the image of God and of the created environment that God declares 'good'. It also speaks of the curvature of the will that turns away from God and in on itself. Consequentially, it speaks of the remaking of the self in a restored human community through the Word who became flesh and who reshapes us by his Spirit. The Christian faith is the telling out of this story in the life of the community so that it not only recalibrates one's perspective but, by drawing us into its story, empowers us to live 'according to the Spirit' in 'life and peace' (Romans 8.5–6).

Not only are the 'immanent ethics' of the people's own limited perspectives and moral powers transcended by divine perspective and power through the Christian story, so are some of the other features of Generation Y that this research uncovers recast in fuller, more satisfying ways. Plans for this day and the next that affect me and mine can become purposes aligned with God's will for the world. The meaning of my life and actions begins to unfold when I decide to travel with Christ and his people on a shared journey that makes sense of who I am and where I am going. Emotional states for which I strive – to be happy, for example – are received as deep gifts of the Spirit as we find ourselves being 'overwhelmed with joy' (Matthew 2.10).

Simon Peter is an early and very interesting case study of someone transformed by the transcending encounter with the kingdom of God in Jesus of Nazareth. His is the story of the formation of an authentic self, a process that includes his renaming: from Simon, he becomes Peter. Through his journey with Jesus he is led into a new quality and quantity of relationships. His brother Andrew and friend Philip become compatriots in the messianic community of which they will both be leaders. The illusion of his brazen confidence in his own powers is repeatedly exposed, whether on the water, in the courtyard or on the mission field and the flaws of his own character are redeemed through patient forgiveness. His ethical perspectives are raised – eventually – from national insularity to universal responsibility. His plans to fish on a Galilean lake for the rest of his life are overtaken by his calling to cast himself out into the ocean of human need. The meaning of his life is revealed in his following of the Christ (John 21.19) and the trials and tribulations that result only reinforce the 'indescribable and glorious joy' (1 Peter 1.8) that he experiences in his transformed self.

The authentic Church and the authentic self of Generation Y

In exploring what it might mean for the self, in a self-limited world, to be transformed into its fullest and most authentic self by the transcending categories of the Christian gospel, we are talking about the raising of humanity to its full stature – the stature that Paul defines as the 'stature of Christ' (Ephesians 4.13). Consistent with Generation Y's best instincts, with their commitment to families (often extended and complex), friendship groups and other social networks, this transformative process takes place in and through others. We can see it in Peter. His encounter with the Christ who would rename him came about through the first community that formed around Jesus; and his particularly intense love of Christ was expressed in the life of the Church. His struggle with the limited capacities of his own powers, community and religion was worked out in the tensions and failings of the early Christian community. His Jewish ethics were reshaped by the evidence of God's inclusion of the Gentiles in the covenant of grace. He discovered that the purpose of his life was to serve the messianic community as elder and apostle. The meaning of his life was found in the mission of the Church. The joy he experienced was a shared experience with others who were also receiving the outcome of their faith, the salvation of their souls (1 Peter 1.9). In short, the forming of his authentic self through his following of Jesus Christ took place within the networks of relationships and responsibilities that we call the Church.

What will the Church of our day look like, and how will it be shaped, if it is to be the sort of community where the selves of members of Generation Y can be more fully and authentically shaped? How is the Church to rise to its full stature, to be the environment in which the transcending categories of the kingdom of God and the empowering capacities of Jesus Christ are present and available for Generation Y?

The true shape of the Church, of course, is Jesus Christ, for the Church is his body. The full stature of the Church, then, is attained in the full stature of Christ. We are the community where Christ is seen and heard, where he is encountered and felt and through whom he acts in the world. We are the community who perform Christ through a set of practices. Putting it the other way around, we are the community through which Jesus manifests his presence and continues his messianic activity.

Among the many practices of the Church, I would like to focus on the Lord's Supper. I do so for three reasons. The first is because it is a core practice of the Church that we have been commanded by Christ to observe. As a core practice, with such clear dominical weight behind it, it is likely that it will be illustrative not only of other practices of the Church but also of the character and identity of the Church itself. The second reason is because the tradition (the *paradosis*) of the Church – that which is passed on – is that there is an intensity of Christ's presence and activity in this particular practice. This is not to imply an exclusivity to the Lord's Supper. What happens here in sacramental concentration happens in other ways and by other means in the life of the Church. But it is to say that Christians across the centuries and cultures of the Church have found the experience of the disciples on the way to Emmaus repeated in their own time, as their eyes have been opened and Christ has been 'made known to them in the breaking of the bread' (Luke 24.31–35). The third reason for choosing the Lord's Supper is because of Jesus' explicit command to 'Do this in remembrance of me' (Luke 22.19). The research into Generation Y has told us a lot about their dislocation and distance from the Christian story. It has also revealed a readiness to hear the story as part of the cultural inheritance, or as the motivation of some of their youth workers, or as a source of wisdom in the face of personal suffering or ethical dilemmas. Furthermore, the research has rightly identified the fragility of many of the values of young people, stretched almost to breaking point from their roots in the Christian story and thus starved of the life and energy they need to survive and to adapt to a changing climate. On the night before Christ died, he told us to do something – he established a practice – by which we are to remember him. What can we learn about the shape of the Church by this practice of the Church?

The Church is deep

The Church is an ancient community that traces its life back to the Day of Pentecost, and then beyond to the birth of Christ, the story of Israel, the exodus of God's people from Egypt, the call of Abraham, the creation of the world and ultimately into the will of God 'before the foundation of the world' (Ephesians 1.4). Jewish prayers at sabbath and Passover remembered God's faithfulness through the ages and his promises for the future, and in remembering they gave thanks. Jesus gave thanks over the bread and wine during his last supper with his disciples as he had done on other occasions during his ministry. Following and expanding this style of prayer, Christians have remembered not only the creation of the world and the history of Israel but also the culmination of both in the coming of Christ and the giving of the Spirit. They too have remembered the promises of God, celebrating those that have come to fruition and looking eagerly forward to their fulfilment in the coming of the kingdom of God's new creation and in the final coming of Christ. And in remembering they have given thanks – hence the prayer by which they do so is traditionally known as the eucharistic prayer, and the Lord's Supper often called the eucharist after the Greek word for thanksgiving.

The Church remembers and give thanks because Jesus, the faithful Jew, remembered and gave thanks, and because he gave explicit instructions to his disciples to do the same. That which the Church does over bread and wine at the Eucharist it does 'at all times and places', as the opening chapter of many of the New Testament letters, with their celebration of praise of the faithfulness of God, bear witness. It is the ancient liturgical pattern of all that precedes the sacramental action. The disciples on the way to Emmaus are downcast but the stranger who draws close to them unfolds the Scriptures to them and their hearts burn within them. The classic shape of the Office style of prayer is a conversation between the reading of Scripture, through which we remember our story, and the singing of songs, by which we respond in praise. The psalms as a collection, and many of them individually, swing from remembrance to praise. Sandwiched between scriptural story and congregational praise in psalm, office, other services of the word and the Eucharist itself, is petition. Having remembered the promises of God and the faithfulness of God, we implore God to remember his promises and to demonstrate his faithfulness, and we give thanks both in anticipation and retrospect for the action of God in our own day.

The Church remembers through signs and times. The signs of the faith – water, oil, book, bread and wine – display the story of the faith; and their foci in Church buildings traditionally make sacred the place of gathering – font, table, lectern. The liturgical year spreads out the story of the faith like a long tapestry that would not be fully seen if it were crushed into one day. The great festivals provide dramatic entry points into the great story of salvation, as we welcome the light at Advent, receive the Word made flesh at Christmas, put sin to death in us over Lent and Holy Week, rise to new life with Christ at Easter, open ourselves to his Spirit at Pentecost.

This list of examples could go on. Suffice it to say at this point that at the centre of the Lord's Supper – a core practice of the Church given by its Lord – is a pattern of remembering and thanking and that, as one would expect of a core practice, its basic rhythm is repeated in the classical structures of the Church's wider worship. The character inscribed on to the Church by this dominical practice is of a *traditioning community* – a community that receives, celebrates and passes on its story in word and action in such a way as to evoke a response of grateful participation.

Earlier we defined the Tradition – that which is passed on – as the gospel of Jesus Christ, which is nothing less than Christ himself. It is important to distinguish this Great Tradition from the lesser traditions by which it is passed on. As we have already seen, this is not an absolute distinction. One of the ways for Paul that the Tradition of Jesus Christ is handed over is in the tradition of the Eucharist. The Apostles' teaching, the fellowship and the prayers are others, as are the apostolic practices of sharing, healing and praise, with everything built upon the foundational action of baptism (Acts 2.37–3.10). Nevertheless, to claim that the Church is the traditioning community charged with making known the story of redemption through certain practices, is not to prescribe exactly how it does so.

Still less is it to insist on secondary practices that may have accrued to the primary practice and which, although they may have clarified for earlier generations, obscure the simplicity of the action for present ones. There is a challenging and deeply theological task here for youth and other Church leaders in a time of cultural change and missionary urgency to make sound judgements between the core and the accretion. It is one to which we shall return later.

There is a specific aspect of the Christian remembering that touches on a theme that the research uncovered in the psyche of Generation Y. It is the theme right at the centre of the Christian memory and the focus of the Lord's Supper in particular: *death*. Jesus gathered his disciples on the night before he would die. He referred to the broken bread as his body, to be given for them, and the cup, from which wine would be poured, as the new covenant in his blood (Luke 22.19–20). On the way to Emmaus the risen Christ explained to the disillusioned disciples that it was 'necessary that the Messiah should suffer these things'

(Luke 24.26). Paul told the Corinthian Christians that 'as often as [they] eat this bread and drink this cup [they] proclaim the Lord's death until he comes' (1 Corinthians 11.26).

Most of Generation Y are bereft of a story to navigate them through death, perhaps more so than any other generation in the history of the world. Even those cultures that had no notion of an afterlife provided a framework of ritual and belief to prepare for death. Yet Generation Y is exposed to images of death (both manufactured and real) on a scale more than any other generation. From hundreds dropping to their deaths from the Twin Towers to bodies buried by the devastating earthquake in Haiti, from executions of kidnapped victims in Iraq to the assisted suicides of the terminally ill, from the frighteningly realistic scenes on films to the savage interactivity of computer games, members of Generation Y have been assailed by the sight of death throughout their lives. They are also the generation most educated in and aware of the ecological death that threatens our planet. And like every generation, they know that one day they will die and so they face the same existential dilemmas about their future destiny and present worth as any generation.

As we know from the research, they are a generation that are by no means dismissive of the paranormal and are open to the veracity of reports and evidence of life beyond death. Intriguingly, many of those who have little contact with the Church at other times will still turn to Christian faith in times of personal loss and societal grief, searching after some way to explain and interpret what has happened to those they have lost. This generation is far more amenable to solemn moments and symbolic means of remembering those who have died than generations immediately preceding them. Internet sites of remembrance and memorial are big business. Schools are adorned with flowers, candles and memorabilia when a student dies. Remembrance Day is having a renaissance with Generation Y. So what might the Christian story have to say to this generation, and what might the eucharistic remembrance have to tell in particular?

First, the Christian story as displayed in the Eucharist is not a theory about life after death but an historical story of a life lived through death. The eucharistic prayer commemorates the life, death and resurrection of an actual person. While data for his life and death can be found in the annals of secular history, evidence for his resurrection is laid out in the continuing Christian experience of his presence in the sacramental action. The story told in the Eucharist moves from memorial of death to manifestation of life. It reports a world which is not limited by death but where death is transcended by life. Moreover, it invites people to step into that world, to 'taste and see that the Lord is good' (Psalm 34.8).

Second, the Christian story provides an explanation of death that is moral as well as mechanical and which takes the reality of evil with full seriousness. This generation is well versed in the interplay between human influence and biological systems. A person's health is harmed through the abuse of drugs, alcohol and even food. Longevity is reduced through deficits of nutrition, clean air, shelter, warmth and affection. International economic systems are brought down through over-borrowing and over-spending, eyes bigger than pockets. The planet's future is threatened through the burning of fossil fuel, nuclear armaments, over-population and over-consumption. The film *Avatar*, among many others, extends humanity's corruptive effect on the environment to other star systems in our galaxy and beyond. The universe itself is threatened by human sin.

The Christian story celebrated in the Eucharist is constructed around damaging effects of human behaviour on the sensitive systems of life created by God and the commitment of God to a new creative process. This regenerating work of God's life-giving Spirit purges those systems of their destructive influences through a new dynamic of life that, in the obedience of the Son, rebalances the human influence on the rest of creation for good rather than evil.

The depth of the purgation which the cosmos needs according to the Christian story told in the Eucharist is not an alien concept to Generation Y, at least if *The Dark Knight*, the second in Christopher Nolan's Batman series of films, is anything to go by. Heath Ledger's rendition of the Joker depicts the sheer 'evilness of evil' (Cocksworth 2009:541). His evil is beyond explanation: he wreaks 'boundless terror and chaos for no reason . . . other than for the sake of terrorising' (Cocksworth 2009:542). He has no other end or satisfaction than exploiting the thin fragility of human pretence at goodness and of maximizing the suffering of the many. The Eucharist agrees with this analysis of the condition in which we find ourselves. It displays Jesus Christ as the victim of this inexplicably destructive evil who became its victor through the one event that evil cannot control – a pure sacrifice of love broken and poured out for the world.

The third reason for being ready to tell confidently the story of death that lies at the heart of the Christian story and is proclaimed in its core practice of the Eucharist, is because the transformation beyond death of which it tells brings a new perspective on life. When one accepts that death is not the end, and that there is more to life than this life and more to creation than this present creation, life here and now begins to look and feel different. This is why I would like to suggest some limits to a tendency in several Christian writers who seek to reappropriate the faith for a post-modern world.[2] Quite properly they want to correct the other-worldly preoccupation of much traditional Christianity, including its evangelical forms, and to make very clear that the gospel calls us to real engagement with this world in order to bring it closer to the character of the kingdom of God. They are providing a much needed ministry to forms of spirituality that reject our God-given responsibility to change this world rather than just wait to be lifted out of it into a timeless heavenly realm. They are right to say the kingdom of God is this creation made new not a parallel creation to which we will one day escape.

At the same time, however, it is important to maintain the perspective of eternity that was so integral to earlier generations of Christians and so much part of their evangelistic zeal. Of course we are not to preach 'pie in the sky when you die', or to scare people into belief, or to disengage from kingdom activity in politics, economics, education and environment. But it is our responsibility to remind people – as the Church of England's traditional Burial Service does – that 'in the midst of life we are in death'. It is our calling to tell the story of the one who made a way through death. And it is our joy to invite others to follow him in the sort of way that they can say with Paul that their hope is to exalt Christ in their bodies whether in life or death (Philippians 1.20). Then their lives will be lived as those who have something to live and die for – Christ's love for the world – and their deaths will be died as those who are ready 'to depart and be with Christ, for that is far better' (Philippians 1.23).

The Church is real

Like a good number of my generation I reacted against many of the practices of the Church, preferring to search out the inner reality of spiritual experience rather than the outer layer of religious observance. What I underestimated was the ease with which this sort of spirituality can slide into the *subjectivization of the spiritual* and the *privatization of the faith*. I failed to see that there are certain means and environments that, in the economy of God, are appointed by Christ to be gifts of his presence and of life in the Spirit. So far in this chapter I have been presenting a case for the Church and its practices to be seen as necessary to the communication of the gospel and its experiences of salvation. The case is both a theological one – *no gospel without the Church*, as we said at the beginning – and also missiological, especially in relation to Generation Y with its urgent need of a traditioning community. At this point, however, it is time to stress the importance of maintaining the dynamic of the Spirit in the disciplines of the Church. The Church is not only a deep body with a long story to tell and certain given ways of telling it. It is also a real body: a body animated by the Spirit of life who is powerfully active in the Church. Indeed, as we also said at the beginning of the chapter, there is *no Church without the Spirit.*

The core practice of the Eucharist illustrates both the Church's dependence upon the Spirit in all its practices and the Spirit's real activity in the Eucharist. The New Testament experience of the Eucharist is that Jesus Christ is made known in the breaking of the bread. There is a real encounter with the real presence of Christ made known by God's Spirit by whom he raised Jesus from the dead (Romans 8.11). Every ministry and practice of the Church is a ministry of the Spirit who gives life (2 Corinthians 3.6). The liturgical acknowledgement of this reality is the invocation of the Spirit, known as the *epiclesis* in the eucharistic prayer. Here the Church calls on the Holy Spirit to manifest and communicate the gift of Jesus' risen life to his people through bread and wine. We call out for the *mediated immediacy* which is the mark of the Holy Spirit's work. The Spirit mediates the presence of Christ to us through the media of the fellowship of the Church and the actions of the Church. Although mediated, the presence of Christ remains immediate because the Spirit is the *Spirit of Christ* and because the actions are the *actions of Christ* through the material he chooses.

Let us unpack these rather condensed claims. First, there is the reality of Christ's presence and, in him, the life of the kingdom of God. Second, there is the communication of his presence and the life of the kingdom through the Spirit of God in whom the risen Christ comes to his people and distributes his gifts. Third, there is the way God reaches material beings like ourselves through material means. The Spirit of God brings Christ and his kingdom to bear upon the world through the activity of people who gather to be built up in his power and go out to transform the world with his love. The building up of the Church and the transformational work of the Church take place through the material means of words and music, bread, wine and water, book, oil and light, hands, legs and hearts.

The way in which the Spirit works remains entirely personal. The reality that the Spirit manifests and communicates is the presence and activity of Christ, hence all the dynamics of personal relationship come into play. It was ever so. The powerful work of the Spirit overshadowing Mary did not disregard her subjectivity. Quite the opposite: it waited for and elicited her obedient response.

This was the supreme moment of God's engagement through the Spirit with the material of creation. God assumes matter, incarnates himself within it, but only with the readiness of Mary to receive that which God was ready to give. The same pattern is replicated in the Eucharist and at other moments in the life of Church where Christ's presence and life is offered to us. Through bread and wine he is really given by the Spirit to be really received in the Spirit. The *givenness* of God's activity in the life of the Church is to be met by the *receptiveness* of the

Church. The readiness to receive involves a range of responsibilities for the Church from an expectation of the Spirit's work in the life and actions of the Church, to facilitation of engagement with the Spirit's work by the planning of worship and mission, to the ongoing formation of hearts that are open to God. Where the Church is able to combine the energies of subjectivity evident in so much of evangelical and charismatic spirituality with the confidence of catholic spirituality in the objectivity of God's action through its life and ministry, it will be the sort of community of authentic faith that is required in order to attract and nurture members of Generation Y.

The Church is true

To be itself, the Church has to be true to itself. Its calling is to be the body of Christ, to be the community where Christ is present and active by his Spirit. We have seen that this involves the Church telling the story of the faith and receiving the reality of the faith, both of which are modelled in the Eucharist in concentrated form. We now turn to another way in which the Church is true to itself, again a character trait that lies at the heart of the Eucharist – the calling to offer itself in obedience.

There are three points in the eucharistic tradition of the churches where the theme of the Church's self-offering has been focused. Eastern Orthodox Churches call the eucharistic prayer itself the *anaphora*, from the Greek for 'carrying up' or 'offering'. It is the great offering of praise for Christ's offering of himself for us. Here the Church offers itself to receive the gift of Christ's presence and to live the life of blessing that his salvation brings. The early Reformed tradition located the offering supremely in the communion itself – 'we present ourselves to this his table ... to eat and drink', said John Knox's *Form of Prayers* (Jasper and Cuming 1980:180). The offering we make is simply the offering of empty hands waiting to be filled with the gift of the Christ who calls us to serve him. The post-Reformation Anglican tradition has placed the moment of offering, or at least its articulation, after the communion. Having heard the story and received the gift of salvation, we offer ourselves to be a 'living sacrifice' and we ask God to 'send us out in the power of the Spirit to live and work to his praise and glory'.

'You are there on the table; you are there in the chalice; you are this body with us, for, collectively, we are this body; we drink of the same chalice because we live the same life', Augustine exhorted his readers in his commentary on the Sermon on the Mount. The coherence of the Christian story and the credibility of its claim to initiate people into the reality of God depends on the capacity of Christian communities to live out the good news of which they speak and to be the body of Christ. We are to embody the kingdom that we have tasted in the new wine of the Eucharist in our common life so that the world looks on and says, 'see how they love one another'. And we are to go and demonstrate the strange power of the kingdom in the world by, as Augustine said again, 'breaking our bread with the hungry'.

The embodiment of the Christian story in the life of the Church and the demonstration of Christian realities through the mission of the Church requires more than Christ shaped believers. It relies upon an institutional shape which itself is shaped by Christ and displays the sort of agility to flourish in different contexts in the sort of ways that bodies adapt to their environments. The history of the Eucharist has some clues to the principles that the Church might apply so that it can change in order to remain itself.

In a moving piece of writing much loved by an earlier generation of liturgists, Gregory Dix concluded his massive study of the origins and development of the Eucharist with a description of the myriad ways in which Christians have obeyed Christ's command to 'do this in remembrance of me'. It was a fitting conclusion to his seminal study which successfully uncovered the basic biblical simplicity of the Eucharist buried under the complexities of the Church's varied liturgies over the centuries. *Taking, thanking, breaking* and *giving* – the original actions of Jesus – is the four-fold shape of the Eucharist, the heart of what we are to do in remembrance of him (Dix 2007). This is the *Rule* of the Church's eucharistic worship – the given, non-negotiable core practices of the core practice. Everything else is *rules* by which we order the songs and prayers, movement and organization, style and character so as to present the core practice to contemporary congregations in ways that are both awesome and accessible.

What is true of the Church's practice of the Eucharist is true for other aspects of its life, especially in a missionary age. How do we identify the core characteristics of the Church's life so that the Church can be true to itself as Christ's body today? Just as Dix and other liturgists in the 20th century delved deeply into the eucharistic traditions to reveal the Christ-shaped structure and movement of the Eucharist, so in the 21st century are we to dig deeply into the core characteristics of the Church's identity so that we can present him to the generations of our nation in awesome and accessible ways?

This piece of research on Generation Y warns us, however, against an ecclesial iconoclasm that fails to represent the texture, light and history of the Church's true self. I am reminded of the tensions with which several British artists wrestled in the 20th century, none more so than John Piper and his art critic wife, Myfanwy. The Pipers were part of the modernist movement in the 1930s that aimed at radical simplicity in art. It sought to abstract the universal characteristics of objects, people and places from the various forms in which they find themselves, and then to express them in lines and colours and shapes. Although Piper was committed to abstract art for several years, producing some notable pieces of art during this period, by the end of the decade he had turned his back on it, deciding that 'Pure abstraction is undernourished' (Spalding 2009:130) and experienced something of a liberation:

> After an abstract period what a release one feels! The avenue at Stadhampton, or the watercress beds at Ewelme are seen with such intensity! But if one abstracts them finally, so that the posts are areas of colour, and the waterfall into the watercress bed becomes like a Ben [Ben Nicolson, a notable abstract artist] relief, then the result can be hung perhaps in Cork Street, but not hung against the human heart. (Spalding 2009:131)

Christian faith cannot be abstracted from the form of the Church and its lived practice. It is not enough simply to say that it is deep and real and true without being able to show a community that is drawing deeply on this story, really experiencing its reality and living out its values truly. It is not even enough, as we saw in Chapter 6, to abstract Christian faith to the principle of *love* without embodying that love in a community that tells the story of love, experiences the source of that love and lives in and from that love in the world. This is the authentic Church that Generation Y, and every generation, has a God-given right to meet and then to hang around its heart.

Notes

Chapter 1 Faith, memory and young people

1. Unchurched refers to those who have no experience of church, dechurched to those who have had some experience but no longer go to church.

2. NCSR – National Centre for Social Research. Original data creators, depositors or copyright holders, the funders of the Data Collections (if different) and the UK Data Archive bear no responsibility for their further analysis or interpretation.

3. Annual Church of England figures for thanksgiving services have varied between 6,000 and 8,000 for the period 2000 to 2007 (Church of England 2009).

4. Interestingly, the Children's Society's Good Childhood Inquiry has picked up on this point. In their report for the inquiry Layard and Dunn (2009) suggest that the loss of ritual following a birth is to be regretted as such ceremonies are important for marking the significance of the event not just for the immediate family but also for wider society. It recommends that where infants are not subject to a religious ceremony at birth a civil one be held instead as a public mark of the parents' commitment to the child.

5. The figure for 2007 includes the Diocese of Europe.

6. The *Teenage Religion and Values Survey* has built up a database of 33,000 young people 13–15 years old.

7. Taking father's lack of employment as an indicator of social deprivation.

8. It is worth noting here that there is sharp separation of the state from religion in France which has affected the opportunities available to the churches to transmit the faith to new generations. Young people in France are less likely to attend church or hold traditional Christian beliefs than their British peers who, for example, routinely experience elements of religion in school (see Chapter 4). Nevertheless, in the 1999 European Values survey 47% of young people (18 to 29 year olds) still said they belonged to a religious denomination, 41% of them Roman Catholic and 2% Protestant (Lambert 2004:32).

9. Beckford (2003:49–50) provides a helpful summary of some of the dimensions of modernization. He describes modernization as 'a complex configuration of

social, legal, economic, political and cultural processes of change that favour [amongst other things] (a) the strengthening of states within an increasingly co-ordinated system of international states; (b) the systematic pursuit of economic productivity and power at national and international levels; (c) the application of theoretical knowledge and practical skills to the enhancement of productivity; (d) the establishment of democratic forms of politics and government; (e) the valorization of education and freedom of thought and expression; (f) the dominance of urban centres of residence and work, and; (g) the cultivation of notions of individual subjectivity, dignity and rights.'

10. Sociologists have used various terms to refer to the development of modernity over the last 50 years – for example 'post-modernity', 'high modernity' or 'late modernity'. They each carry theoretical implications beyond the scope of the current discussion. We refer to late modernity in this book to indicate that while society has undergone far-reaching socio-economic change, particularly in relation to information and communications technology, we see these changes as a continuity of, rather than break with, modernity and many structural determinants of social life persist for young people (see Furlong and Cartmel 2007:1–12).

11. Since this chapter was written, Voas and Ling (2010:66) have noted that in 2009 the Muslim population was 2.5 million.

12. *Making Sense of Generation Y* and the current study have intellectual continuity, but are independent studies and different young people took part in each.

Chapter 2 Mission and method

1. See their website http://www.scriptureunion.org.uk/8.id

2. Information sourced from Youthwork Magazine, *We Love Our Youth Worker! The national charter for church youth workers*, Youth Work and Amaze, www.weloveouryouthworker.org.uk/pdf/charter_introductory_booklet.pdf

3. See www.centreforyouthministry.ac.uk for further details.

4. See http://www.oasisuk.org/uk/projects/academies for details.

5. Search undertaken on 29 August 2009; this is 16,000 more than the first search undertaken seven months earlier.

6. See http://www.fyt.org.uk/userpdfs/b1b47a07566020d6e574.pdf for a research report on this campaign.

7. The Centre for Youth Ministry was established with this approach to training. Students and graduates affirm the benefits of the ongoing possibilities of letting theory inform practice and practice experience inform understandings of theory.

8. The denominational orientation of the youth work projects were either mainstream Protestant or non-specific. We were unable to include any Roman Catholic projects in the study.

Chapter 3 Bedroom spirituality

1. Guilt relates to the morality of an action. It is a feeling engendered in the individual when she recognizes she has *done* something wrong. Shame refers more directly to the self and its inadequacies. It is a feeling engendered when the individual recognizes herself as *being* something wrong.
2. There was a significant difference in our sample between frequent and infrequent churchgoers' perception of home. 62% of frequent churchgoers indicated in the survey that their home was somewhere they felt 'secure and loved' compared to 54% of infrequent churchgoers. 29% of infrequent churchgoers agreed with the statement 'at home I sometimes feel loved, other times I don't' compared to just 13% of frequent churchgoers.
3. In terms of self-perception, 76% of frequent churchgoers and 64% of infrequent churchgoers described themselves as 'somebody you can trust'.
4. When asked if the youth club made them feel differently about themselves, 75% of the young people indicated 'happier', 57% 'more friendly', 51% 'more confident', 39% 'more loved', 32% 'more motivated', 23% 'more peaceful' and 21% 'more responsible'.
5. 95% of frequent churchgoers said the same.
6. This section is an edited version of Collins-Mayo 2008.
7. Prayer is also important among the adult population (see Barley 2006:7–8, 41–45).

Chapter 4 Lost in transmission

1. Of the frequent churchgoers, 8% described themselves as 'spiritual', 27% as 'religious' and 19% as 'religious and spiritual'.
2. This left 20% agnostic, 11% atheist and 24% who didn't know what they were.
3. Although exemption to the nature of worship can be applied for.
4. Mellor (2007: 595) makes this point in relation to the sacred in his commentary on Archer's (2000) work.
5. Only one club was based in an area where there was a history of sectarian divide.

Chapter 9 Authentic Church

1. Page 82.
2. For example Marcus J. Borg (1997), *The God We Never Knew: Beyond dogmatic religion to a more authentic contemporary faith*, New York: HarperCollins.

Bibliography

Roland Allen (1985) *Missionary Methods: St Paul's or Ours*, Grand Rapids: Eerdmans Publishing.

Nancy Ammerman (ed.) (2007) 'Introduction', *Everyday Religion: Observing Modern Religious Lives*, New York: Oxford University Press, pp. 3–18.

Nancy Ammerman (2006) 'Journeys of Faith: Meeting the Challenges in Twenty-First-Century America', in James Heft (ed.), *Passing On The Faith: Transforming Traditions for the Next Generation of Jews, Christians, and Muslims*, New York: Fordham University Press, pp. 37–51.

Margaret S. Archer (2000) *Being Human*, Cambridge: Cambridge University Press.

Mark Ashton (1986) *Christian Youth Work*, Eastbourne: Kingsway, p. 68.

Jacinta Ashworth and Ian Farthing (2007) *Churchgoing in the UK: A Research Report from Tearfund on Church Attendance in the UK*, Teddington: Tearfund.

Lynda Barley (2006) *Time to Listen: Christian Roots, Contemporary Spirituality*, London: Church House Publishing.

BBC News (2009) 'Nurse Suspended for Prayer Offer', 1 February, http://news.bbc.co.uk/1/hi/england/somerset/7863699.stm

BBC News (2008) 'Sharia Law in UK is "Unavoidable" ', 7 February, http://news.bbc.co.uk/1/hi/uk/7232661.stm

BBC News (2006) 'Cross Row Stokes Christian Anger', 15 October, http://news.bbc.co.uk/1/hi/uk/6051486.stm

Ed Beavan (2009) 'Knowledge of Bible Stories Declines', *Church Times*, 17 July.

Ulrich Beck and Elisabeth Beck-Gernsheim (2002) *Individualization*, London: Sage.

Elisabeth Beck-Gernsheim (2002) *Reinventing the Family: In Search of New Lifestyles*, Cambridge: Polity.

James A. Beckford (2003) *Social Theory and Religion*, Cambridge: Cambridge University Press.

Andy Bennett (2000) *Popular Music and Youth Culture: Music, Identity and Place*, Basingstoke: Macmillan.

Peter L. Berger, Brigitte Berger and Hansfried Kellner (1974) *The Homeless Mind*, Harmondsworth: Penguin.

David Bosch (1991) *Transforming Mission: Paradigm Shifts in Theology of Mission*, New York: Orbis.

John P. Bowen (2009) ' "What Happened Next?" Vincent Donovan Thirty-Five Years On', *International Bulletin of Missionary Research*, pp. 79–82.

Mike Breen (1993) *Outside In*, London: Scripture Union.

Danny Brierley (2003) *Joined Up*, Carlisle: Authentic Lifestyle.

Peter Brierley (2006) *Pulling Out of the Nose Dive*, London: Christian Research.

Peter Brierley (ed.) (2008) *UK Christian Handbook: Religious Trends 7*, Swindon: Christian Research.

Steve Bruce (2001) 'The Social Process of Secularization', in Richard K. Fenn (ed.), *The Blackwell Companion To Sociology Of Religion*, Malden, MA: Blackwell, pp. 249–63.

Walter Brueggeman, (1986) *Hopeful Imagination*, Philadelphia: Fortress Press.

Walter Brueggemann (2002) *The Land: Place as Gift, Promise, and Challenge in Biblical Faith*, Minneapolis: Augsburg Fortress.

Church of England (1996) *Youth A Part*, London: National Society/Church House Publishing.

Church of England (2006) *Promoting a Safe Church: Policy for Safeguarding Adults in the Church of England*, London: Church House Publishing.

Church of England (2007) *Research Towards Fresh Expressions Of Church*, http://www.cofe.anglican.org/info/statistics/churchstats2005/freshexpression0207.htm

Church of England (2008), *Church Statistics 2006/7*, http://www.cofe.anglican.org/info/statistics/churchstats2006/statisticspg11b.htm

Church of England (2009) *Church Statistics 2007/8*, http://www.cofe.anglican.org/info/statistics/churchstats2007/statisticscontent.html

Catherine Clark, Amrita Ghosh, Emrys Green and Naushin Shariff (2008) *Media Portrayal of Young People – Impact and Influences*, London: National Children's Bureau.

Ashley Cocksworth (2009) 'The Dark Knight and the Evilness of Evil', in *The Expository Times*, 120.11, pp. 541–3.

Christopher Cocksworth (2008) *Holding Together: Gospel, Church and Spirit – The Essentials of Christian Identity*, Norwich: Canterbury Press.

Sylvia Collins (1997) *Young People's Faith in Late Modernity*, PhD Thesis, Guildford: University of Surrey.

Sylvia Collins-Mayo (2008) 'Young People's Spirituality and the Meaning of Prayer', in Abby Day (ed.), *Religion and the Individual*, Aldershot: Ashgate, pp. 33–45.

Murray Cox (1990) 'Psychopathology and Treatment of Psychotic Aggression', in Robert Bluglass and Paul Bowden (eds), *Principles and Practice of Forensic Psychiatry*, London: Churchill Livingstone.

Stephen Croft (2008a) 'What Counts As A Fresh Expression Of Church And Who Decides?', in Louise Nelstrop and Martin Percy (eds), *Evaluating Fresh Expressions*, Norwich: Canterbury Press.

Stephen Croft (2008b) *Mission Shaped Questions*, London: Church House Publishing.

Abby Day (2010) ' "Believing in Belonging": an exploration of young people's social contexts and constructions of belief', in Sylvia Collins-Mayo and Pink Dandelion (eds), *Religion and Youth*, Aldershot: Ashgate.

Grace Davie (1993) 'Believing Without Belonging: A Liverpool Case Study', *Archives de Sciences Sociales des Religions*, Vol 38, No 81, pp. 79–89.

Grace Davie (2000) *Religion in Modern Europe: A Memory Mutates*, Oxford: Oxford University Press.

Grace Davie (2007a) 'Vicarious Religion: A methodological challenge', in Nancy Ammerman (ed.), *Everyday Religion: Observing Modern Religious Lives*, New York: Oxford University Press, pp. 21–35.

Grace Davie (2007b) *The Sociology of Religion*, London: Sage.

Bernard Davies (1999) *From Thatcherism to New Labour: A History of the Youth Service in England Vol 2*. Leicester: NYA.

Kendra Creasy Dean (2004) *Practicing Passion*, Grand Rapids: Eerdmans.

Dom Gregory Dix (2007) *The Shape of the Liturgy*, London: Continuum.

Vincent J. Donovan (1982) *Christianity Rediscovered: An Epistle From the Masai*, London: SCM.

John Drane (2008) *After McDonaldization: Mission, Ministry and Christian Discipleship in an Age of Uncertainty*, Grand Rapids: Baker Academic.

John Drane and Olive M. Fleming Drane (2004) *Family Fortunes*, London: Darton, Longman & Todd.

Simon Duncan and Miranda Phillips (2008) 'New Families? Tradition and change in modern relationships', in Alison Park et al. (eds), (2008) *British Social Attitudes: The 24th Report*, London: Sage.

Robert Emmons (2001) 'Making a science of virtue', *Science and Theology News Online Edition*, www.stnews.org/News-2301.htm, January 1

Michel Foucault (1990) *The History of Sexuality, Vol 1: An Introduction*. Trans. Robert Hurley, New York: Random House (first published in 1978).

Kate Fox (2004) *Watching The English: The Hidden Rules of English Behaviour*, London: Hodder and Stoughton.

Leslie J. Francis (1990) 'The Religious Significance of Denominational Identity

Among Eleven Year Old Children in England', *Journal of Christian Education*, Vol 97, pp. 23–8.

Leslie J. Francis (2001) *The Values Debate: A Voice from the Pupils*, London: Woburn Press.

Leslie J. Francis and Mandy Robbins (2005) *Urban Hope and Spiritual Health: The Adolescent Voice*, Werrington: Epworth.

Leslie J. Francis and Mandy Robbins (2006) 'Prayer, purpose in life, personality and social attitudes among non-churchgoing 13- to 15-year-olds in England and Wales', *Research in the Social Scientific Study of Religion*, Vol 17, pp. 123–56.

Francis Fukuyama (1992) *The End of History and the Last Man*, New York: Free Press.

Andy Furlong and Fred Cartmel (2007) *Young People and Social Change: New Perspectives*, Maidenhead: McGraw-Hill and Open University Press.

Robin Gamble (2006) 'Doing traditional church really well', in Stephen Croft (ed.), *The Future of the Parish System*, London: Church House Publishing.

Caroline Gammell (2009) 'Primary school receptionist "Facing Sack" after daughter talks about Jesus to classmate', *Telegraph.co.uk*, 11 February, www.telegraph.co.uk/news/newstopics/religion/4590870/Primary-school-receptionist-facing-sack-after-daughter-talks-about-Jesus-to-classmate.html

Jason Gardner (2008) *Mend The Gap: Can the Church Reconnect the Generations?*, Leicester: IVP.

Anthony Giddens (1991) *Modernity and Self-Identity: Self and Society in the Late Modern Age*, Cambridge: Polity Press.

Maxine Green (2006) *A Journey of Discovery: Spirituality and Spiritual Development in Youth Work*, Leicester: National Youth Agency.

C. Kirk Hadaway, Penny Long Marler and Mark Chaves (1993) 'What the polls don't show: A closer look at US church attendance', *American Sociological Review*, 58, pp. 741–52.

David Harvey (1993) 'From space to place and back again: reflections on the condition of postmodernity', in John Bird et al. (eds), *Mapping the Futures: Local Cultures and Global Change*, London, Routledge, pp. 3–29.

Stanley Hauerwas (1981a) *A Community of Character: Towards a Constructive Christian Social Ethic*, Notre Dame: University of Notre Dame Press.

Stanley Hauerwas (1981b) *Vision And Virtue: Essays in Christian Ethical Reflection*, Notre Dame: University of Notre Dame Press.

Stanley Hauerwas (1983) 'The Servant Community: Christian Social Ethics', in John Berkman and Michael Cartwright (eds), (2001) *The Hauerwas Reader*, Durham, NC: Duke University Press.

Stanley Hauerwas (1985) *Against the Nations: War and Survival in a Liberal Society*, Notre Dame: University of Notre Dame Press.

Stanley Hauerwas (1993) 'The interpretation of Scripture: why discipleship is required', in John Berkman and Michael Cartwright (eds), (2001) *The Hauerwas Reader*, Durham, NC: Duke University Press.

Paul Heelas and Linda Woodhead (2005) *The Spiritual Revolution: Why Religion is Giving Way to Spirituality*, Oxford: Blackwell Publishing.

Danièle Hervieu-Léger (2001) 'Individualism and the validation of faith', in Richard K. Fenn (ed.), *The Blackwell Companion to Sociology of Religion*, Malden, MA: Blackwell, pp. 161–75.

Danièle Hervieu-Léger (2000) *Religion as a Chain of Memory*, Cambridge: Polity Press.

Andrew Hough (2009) 'Vicar Attacks "Princess Diana Funeral Culture" for Pop Songs at Funerals', http://www.telegraph.co.uk/news/newstopics/religion/6453463/Vicar-attacks-Princess-Diana-funeral-culture-for-pop-songs-at   -funerals.html

John Hull (2008) 'Mission-shaped and kingdom focused', in Stephen Croft (ed.), *Mission-Shaped Questions*, London: Church House Publishing.

John Inge (2003) *A Christian Theology of Place*, Aldershot: Ashgate.

Kandy James (2001) ' "I just gotta have my own space!" The bedroom as a leisure site for adolescent girls', *Journal Of Leisure Research*, Vol. 33, No 1, pp. 71–90.

Bibliography

Alan Jamieson (2002) *Churchless Faith*, London: SPCK.

Leonard A. Jason (1997) *Community Building*, Westport: Praeger.

R. C. D. Jasper and G. J. Cuming (eds) (1980) *Prayers of the Eucharist: Early and Reformed*, New York: Oxford University Press.

Philip Jenkins (2007) *God's Continent: Christianity, Islam and Europe's Religious Crisis*, Oxford: Oxford University Press.

William Kay and Leslie J. Francis (1996) *Drift from the Churches: Attitude toward Christianity during Childhood and Adolescence*, Cardiff: University of Wales Press.

Yves Lambert (2004) 'A turning point in religious evolution in Europe', *Journal of Contemporary Religion*, Vol. 19, No 1, pp. 29–45.

Richard Layard and Judy Dunn (2009) *A Good Childhood: Searching for Values in a Competitive Age*, London: Penguin.

Sian Lincoln (2005) 'Feeling the noise: teenagers, bedrooms and music', *Leisure Studies*, Vol. 24, pp. 399–414.

Alasdair MacIntyre (2000, first published 1981) *After Virtue*, London: Duckworth.

Dave Male (2008) 'Who are Fresh Expressions really for? Do they really reach the unchurched?', in Louise Nelstrop and Martin Percy (eds), *Evaluating Fresh Expressions*, Norwich: Canterbury Press.

Julia Margo and Mike Dixon with Nick Pearce and Howard Reed (2006) *Freedom's Orphans: Raising Youth in a Changing World*, London: IPPR.

David Martin (2002) 'Alternative visions and constraints: Religious Education', in *Christian Language And Its Mutations: Essays in Sociological Understanding*, Aldershot: Ashgate, pp. 135–44.

Ed Mayo and Agnes Nairn (2009) *Consumer Kids: How Big Business is Grooming our Children for Profit*, London: Constable.

Philip Mellor (2007) 'Embodiment, emotion and religious experience: religion, culture and the charismatic body', in James A. Beckford and N. J. Demerath III (eds), *The Sage Handbook of Religion*, London: Sage, pp. 587–607.

Sven Mørch and Helle Andersen (2006) 'Individualization and the changing youth life', in Carmen Leccardi and Elisabetta Ruspini (eds), *A New Youth? Young People, Generations and Family Life*, Aldershot: Ashgate.

Bernard Moss (2005) *Religion and Spirituality*, Lyme Regis: Russell House Publishing.

Sally Nash (2009) 'Sacralised Youth Work', *Journal of Youth and Theology*, Vol. 8 No 2, pp. 22–40.

Sally Nash, Sylvia Collins-Mayo and Bob Mayo (2007) 'Raising Christian consciousness: creating place', *Journal of Youth and Theology*, Vol. 6, No 2, pp. 41–59.

National Youth Agency (2007) *The Contribution of Youth Work to the Every Child Matters Outcomes*, Leicester: National Youth Agency.

NCSR (National Centre for Social Research) (2008) [computer file], *British Social Attitudes Survey*, Colchester: UK Data Archive [distributor], April 2008, SN:5823.

Lesslie Newbigin (1989) *The Gospel in a Pluralist Society*, London: SPCK.

nfpSynergy (2007) *Typical Young People: A Study of What Young People are Really Like Today*, London: nfpSynergy.

Jonathan Oloyede (2005) 'Black Majority', *Christianity*, October, p. 26 in Brierley, 2006:105.

ONS (Office for National Statistics) (2004a) 'Age and Sex Distribution: Muslim population is youngest', http://www.statistics.gov.uk/cci/nugget.asp?id=955

ONS (Office for National Statistics) (2004b) 'Religious Populations: Christianity is main religion in Britain', http://www.statistics.gov.uk/cci/nugget.asp?id=954

ONS (Office for National Statistics) (2006) *Focus on Religion*, http://www.statistics.gov.uk/focuson/religion/

ONS (Office for National Statistics) (2009a) 'Marriages (Provisional) Selected Data Tables, England and Wales, Table 1: Summary of Marriages' http://www.statistics.gov.uk/statbase/Product.asp?vlnk=14275

ONS (Office for National Statistics) (2009b) 'Life Expectancy', http://www.statistics.gov.uk/cci/nugget.asp?ID=168

Kenneth I. Pargament and Mark S. Rye (1998) 'Forgiveness as a method of religious coping', in Everett L. Worthington Jr (ed.), *Dimensions Of Forgiveness*, Philadelphia: Templeton Foundation Press, pp. 62–3.

Alison Park et al. (eds) (2008) *British Social Attitudes: The 24th Report*, London: Sage.

Martyn Percy (2006) 'Many rooms in my Father's house: The changing identity of the English parish church', in Stephen Croft (ed.), *The Future of the Parish System*, London: Church House Publishing.

Michael Polanyi (1983, first published in 1958) *Personal Knowledge: Towards a Post-critical Philosophy*, London: Routledge and Kegan Paul.

John Pollock (1959) *The Good Seed: The Story of the Children's Special Service Mission and the Scripture Union*, London: Hodder and Stoughton.

Phil Rankin (2005) *Buried Spirituality*, Salisbury: Sarum College Press.

Philip Richter and Leslie J. Francis (1998) *Gone But Not Forgotten: Church Leaving and Returning*, London: Darton, Longman & Todd.

Carl Rogers (1980) *A Way of Being*, Boston, MA: Houghton Mifflin.

Malcolm Ruel (1982) 'Christians as believers', in John Davis (ed.), *Religious Organization and Religious Experience*, ASA Monograph 21, London: Academic, pp. 9–31.

Sara Savage, Sylvia Collins-Mayo, Bob Mayo with Graham Cray (2006) *Making Sense of Generation Y: The Worldview of 15- to 25-year-olds*, London: Church House Publishing.

Nicholas Shepherd (2009) *Trying to be Christian: A Qualitative Study of Young People's Participation in Two Youth Ministry Projects*, PhD Thesis, King's College London.

Georg Simmel (1950) 'Faithfulness and gratitude', in Kurt H. Wolff (ed. and trans.), *The Sociology of Georg Simmel*, New York: Free Press, pp. 379–95.

Anita Singh (2009) 'Pop tunes eclipse hymns at British funerals', www.telegraph.co.uk/culture/music

Christian Smith with Melinda Lundquist Denton (2005) *Soul Searching: The Religious and Spiritual Lives of American Teenagers*, New York: Oxford University Press.

Frances Spalding (2009) *John Piper, Myfanwy Piper: Lives in Art*, Oxford: Oxford University Press.

Mark Sturge (2005) *Look What The Lord Has Done!*, Bletchley: Scripture Union.

Loraine Sweeney (2008) *Your Shout: The Views of Young People Living in Poor Communities in North East England*, Newcastle Upon Tyne: IPPR North.

Charles Taylor (1991) *The Ethics of Authenticity*, Cambridge, MA: Harvard University Press.

John Taylor (1972) *The Go-Between God*, London: SCM Press.

Teachernet (2009) 'Faith Schools', www.teachernet.gov.uk/wholeschool/faith schools/

John B. Thompson (2003) *The Ecclesiology of Stanley Hauerwas*, Aldershot: Ashgate.

Angela Tilby (2008) 'What question does Catholic ecclesiology pose for contemporary mission and Fresh Expressions?', in Stephen Croft (ed.), *Mission Shaped Questions*, London: Church House Publishing.

Paul Tillich (1951) *Systematic Theology*, Chicago: University of Chicago Press.

Paul Tillich (1962) *The Courage To Be*, London: Fontana Library.

Graham Tomlin (2008) 'Can we develop churches that can transform the culture?', in Stephen Croft (ed.), *Mission-Shaped Questions*, London: Church House Publishing.

UNICEF, (2007) Child Poverty in Perspective: An Overview of Child Well-being in Rich Countries, Florence: UNICEF Innocenti Research Centre.

Giselle Vincett and Sylvia Collins-Mayo (2010) '(Dis)Engagements with Christianity amongst young people in England and Scotland', *Annual Review of the Sociology of Religion*.

David Voas (2003) 'Is Britain a Christian country?', in Paul Avis (ed.), *Public Faith?*, London: SPCK, pp. 92–105.

David Voas (2009) 'The rise and fall of fuzzy fidelity in Europe', *European Sociological Review*, Vol. 25, No 2, pp. 155–68.

David Voas and Alasdair Crockett (2005) 'Religion in Britain: neither believing nor belonging', *Sociology*, Vol. 39 No 1, pp. 11–28.

David Voas and Rodney Ling (2010) 'Religion in Britain and the United States', in Alison Park et al., *British Social Attitudes, The 26th Report*, London: Sage.

Tony Walter (ed.) (1999) *The Mourning for Diana*, Oxford: Berg.

Pete Ward (1996) *Growing Up Evangelical*, London: SPCK.

Pete Ward (1997) *Youthwork and the Mission of God*, London: SPCK.

Martin Warner (2008) 'How does a mixed economy church connect with contemporary spirituality?', in Stephen Croft (ed.), *Mission-Shaped Questions*, London: Church House Publishing.

Simone Weil (1952) *The Need for Roots*, London: Routledge & Kegan Paul.

David Wilkinson (2008) 'What are the lessons from evangelism and apologetics for new communities?', in Stephen Croft (ed.), *Mission-Shaped Questions*, London: Church House Publishing.

Rowan Williams (2008) *Dostoevsky: Language, Faith And Fiction*, London: Continuum.

Rowan Williams (2010) Address on 5 March 'Changing the landscape: fresh expressions and the long term', www.freshexpressions.org.uk/training/lincoln

Bryan Wilson (1982) *Religion in Sociological Perspective*, Oxford: Oxford University Press.

Kay Withers and Ruth Sheldon (2008) *Behind the Screen*, London: IPPR.

YouGov (2007) 'Attitudes To Religion' http://www.yougov.co.uk/extranets/ygarchives/content/pdf/Humphrys%20Religion%20Questions.pdf

Kerry Young (1999) *The Art of Youth Work*, Lyme Regis: Russell House Publishing.

Index

Making Sense of Generation Y
The world view of 15- 25-year-olds
Sara Savage, Sylvia Collins-Mayo, Bob Mayo with Graham Cray

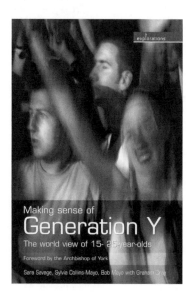

978 0 7151 4051 2   234 x 156mm   224pp   £12.99

For Generation Y, born after 1982, Margaret Thatcher is a piece of social history, relationships happen over the internet and music marks their territory. How does this generation think about the world? What does their spirituality look like? And what implications does this have for the Church?

Making Sense of Generation Y addresses the urgent need for the Church to re-connect with young people in today's society, and to communicate with them in a way they can understand.

Through researching the relationship young people aged 15 to 25 have to the popular arts (soaps, film, music, clubbing, advertising and culturally iconic images), the authors explore the implications of their worldview for youth work and youth ministry as well as the wider church.

 CHURCH HOUSE PUBLISHING

Available from all good bookshops
or direct from Church House Publishing
Tel: + 44 (0)1603 785925   www.chpublishing.co.uk